Published by The Book Chief Publi
(a trademark under Lydian Group Ltd)
Suite 2A, Blackthorn House, St Paul's Square,
Birmingham, B3 1RL
www.thebookchief.com

The moral right of the author has been asserted.

Text Copyright © 2024 by **Bernadette Ashton**

All rights reserved. No part of this book may be reproduced, stored in a retrieval system, or transmitted in any form or by any means, electronic, mechanical, photocopying, recording, public performances or otherwise, without written permission of **Bernadette Ashton**, except for brief quotations embodied in critical articles or reviews. The book is for personal and commercial use by the Author **Bernadette Ashton.**

The right of **Bernadette Ashton** to be identified as the author of this work has been asserted in accordance with sections 77 and 78 of the copyright Designs and Patents Act 1988.

Book Cover Design: Deearo Marketing
Editing: Sharon Brown
Typesetting / Proofreading: Sharon Brown
Publishing: Sharon Brown

THE BOOK CHIEF®
IGNITE YOUR WRITING

LIVING WITH ADULT ADHD

Embracing The Chaos With A Smile

By Bernadette Ashton

ADHD Lancashire

Table of Contents

DEDICATION 9
ACKNOWLEDGEMENTS 11
FOREWORD 15
   By Andrea Bilbow OBE 15
CHAPTER 1 17
   NAVIGATING NEURODIVERSITY: A PERSONAL AND PROFESSIONAL JOURNEY . 17
      By Bernadette Ashton 17
CHAPTER 2 25
   LIFE IS NOT WHERE YOU START... 25
      By Peter Aldcroft-Colling 25
CHAPTER 3 33
   TO THE TEEN WHO STRUGGLES TO FEEL ACCEPTED 33
      By Rachael Beattie 33
CHAPTER 4 39
   HOW THE HELL DID I GET HERE? 39
      By Jen Bee 39
CHAPTER 5 45
   FROM MESS TO SUCCESS: THE BUMPY ROAD TO REACHING MY POTENTIAL . 45
      By Alan P Brown 45
CHAPTER 6 51
   MY ADHD JOURNEY 51
      By Alison Clink 51
CHAPTER 7 57
   LIKE A PANTOMIME HORSE, BUT DRUNK 57
      By Tony Coward 57
CHAPTER 8 67
   TURNING TIDES: A TALE OF ADDICTION, ADHD AND TRANSFORMATIVE COACHING 67
      By James Hansen 67
CHAPTER 9 73
   DIFFERENCE IN THE MAKING 73
      By Jan Hanson 73
CHAPTER 10 79

LATE DIAGNOSED, WITH A LOVE FOR LIFE AND INSPIRING OTHERS 79
  By Jenny Haslam 79
CHAPTER 11 .... **87**
  MY NEW ROLE AS ME! 87
    By Natasha Hickling 87
CHAPTER 12 .... **95**
  EMBRACING MY ADHD 95
    By Beverley Nolker 95
CHAPTER 13 .... **103**
  BECOMING ATTENTIVE 103
    By Chris Maddocks 103
CHAPTER 14 .... **111**
  MY JOURNEY WITH ADHD 111
    By Steven McLaughlin 111
CHAPTER 15 .... **119**
  MOTIVATE THE MIND 119
    By Emily Nuttall 119
CHAPTER 16 .... **125**
  ADHDTASTIC™: CRAFTING A LIFE THAT ALIGNS WITH MY ADHD 125
    By Kimberley B. Pereira 125
CHAPTER 17 .... **133**
  LAUGHING THROUGH THE CHAOS: MY ADHD JOURNEY 133
    By Robert Powell 133
CHAPTER 18 .... **141**
  ADHD AND MY JOURNEY TO SELF-ACCEPTANCE 141
    By Emma Sails 141
CHAPTER 19 .... **147**
  PARTY GIRL ADHD SUCCESS 147
    By Kim Sheppard 147
CHAPTER 20 .... **153**
  RELATABLE & LAUGHABLE: A ROLLERCOASTER OF AN ADHD EXPERIENCE. 153
    By Beth Thomas 153
CHAPTER 21 .... **161**
  THE ADHD REALISATION 161
    By Emma Whalley 161
SHORT STORIES **169**

CONTRIBUTORS TO THE BOOK	**169**
NEW START	**171**
By Rebecca Batstone	*171*
PAUL'S QUIRKY FUNERAL PROCESSION	**173**
By Paul Carter	*173*
CONFUSING FRENCH LESSON	**175**
By Paul Carter	*175*
FINDING MYSELF: FROM CAREER UNCERTAINTY TO ADHD DIAGNOSIS	**177**
By Andy Gonzalez	*177*
LIFE HAPPENS WHEN YOU LEAST EXPECT IT	**181**
By Cynthia Hammer	*181*
ADHD & DRAMA SUCCESS	**185**
By Abi Horsfield	*185*
MY DIAGNOSIS TRANSFORMED MY LIFE	**187**
By Daley Jones	*187*
ADHD, PTSD AND MY MILITARY CAREER	**189**
By Carlos Rodriguez	*189*
ADHD: UNLEASHING LIFE'S POTENTIAL	**191**
By Liam Tuohy	*191*
EPILOGUE	**193**
DIRECTORY OF CO-AUTHORS AND CONTRIBUTORS	**195**
ABOUT THE CREATOR OF THIS BOOK	**199**
ADHD LANCASHIRE SERVICES	**205**

- Ben Ashton -

Dedication

This book is dedicated with boundless love and profound admiration to my son, whose insatiable curiosity ignited my exploration of the world of ADHD over 18 years ago. Your unyielding curiosity and zest for life have been, and continue to be, a constant source of inspiration throughout my life's journey.

Your boundless energy, mischievous spirit, and occasional pranks keep me on my toes, reminding me of the joys and surprises life has to offer. Your unique way of experiencing the world has deepened my understanding of ADHD and kindled a fire within me to advocate for awareness and understanding.

My love and admiration for you only deepen as you grow and thrive. You are a constant reminder of the incredible resilience and potential that individuals with ADHD possess. I dedicate this book to you, my beloved son, with all my heart, and I thank you for being the driving force behind my quest to shed light on this remarkable journey.

With all my love and appreciation,

Mum.

Acknowledgements

We find ourselves at the culmination of an extraordinary journey marked by the generosity, expertise, and unwavering support of numerous individuals who, like us, navigate the world with adult ADHD. We acknowledge with profound gratitude the collective contributions that have breathed life into this book.

First and foremost, we extend our heartfelt thanks to our co-authors, whose unique collaborative spirit and unwavering dedication have been the bedrock of this endeavour. Your personal journeys, filled with trials and triumphs, are deeply touching and will undoubtedly resonate with the countless adults following a similar path. Each of you has brought a unique perspective and profound insight to the stories shared within these pages, and for your unwavering creativity and camaraderie, we are immensely grateful.

To the individuals who have generously shared their poignant short stories, your willingness to provide glimpses into the inner workings of your personal experiences. Your candour and openness have made this project resonate deeply, and we hold your voices in the highest regard.

We reserve a special place in our hearts for Andrea Bilbow OBE, and we want to express our deepest gratitude for her remarkable contribution to this project. Her eloquent foreword is an inspiring prelude to the captivating tales unfolding within these pages. Andrea's dedication to supporting families and adults with ADHD for nearly three decades is extraordinary. It is a testament to her unwavering commitment to positively impacting the lives of those affected by ADHD.

We feel truly honoured to have her as an integral part of this journey.

Her expertise, advocacy, and tireless efforts in the field have raised awareness and provided invaluable support and resources to countless individuals and families. We are deeply grateful for your unwavering support and the inspiration to foster understanding and empathy for those living with ADHD.

This book is dedicated with boundless love and profound admiration to my son, whose insatiable curiosity ignited my exploration of the world of ADHD over 18 years ago. Your unyielding curiosity and zest for life have been, and continue to be, a constant source of inspiration throughout my life's journey. Your boundless energy, mischievous spirit, and occasional pranks keep me on my toes, reminding me of the joys and surprises life has to offer. Your unique way of experiencing the world has deepened my understanding of ADHD and kindled a fire within me to advocate for awareness and understanding.

Our sincerest appreciation extends to our editor, whose meticulous guidance and editorial finesse have skillfully woven our words into a seamless and powerful narrative. Your dedication to refining our work has not gone unnoticed, and we are deeply thankful for your invaluable contributions.

To our support group members, both past and present, your unwavering encouragement and shared camaraderie planted the seed that grew into the creation of this book. The laughter, understanding, and stories we've shared have woven a tapestry of friendship that forms the beating heart of this work.

Lastly, to our readers, who embark on this literary adventure with open hearts and minds, your engagement with these stories breathes life into our words.

Your insatiable curiosity fuels our motivation to continue sharing narratives, bridging understanding and fostering empathy.

With the deepest appreciation, Bernadette Ashton

Foreword

By Andrea Bilbow OBE

Founder and CEO of ADDISS

Welcome to a journey filled with laughter, resilience, and the vibrant spirit of those who have dared to embrace life with ADHD – a journey masterfully chronicled by the talented co-authors of this delightful book, to a world where chaos reigns supreme, the mundane becomes extraordinary, and the absurdity of life takes centre stage. Yes, you've ventured into the realm of Adult ADHD – a place where the focus is as fleeting as a soap bubble on a windy day and where the organisation is a concept as foreign as ancient hieroglyphs.

What strikes me most about this book is the courage of the co-authors in sharing their personal anecdotes. Each story is a testament to the strength found in embracing the chaos that comes with ADHD. It's a celebration of quirks, a recognition of the beauty within the unconventional, and a reminder that humour can be a powerful ally in facing the twists and turns of life.

Prepare yourself for tales of forgetting keys in the fridge, embarking on a mission to clean the house only to rearrange the sock drawer alphabetically, and attempting to follow a recipe that somehow turns into an impromptu science experiment. These stories aren't just anecdotes; they're windows into the wonderfully chaotic minds of those living with Adult ADHD.

As you turn the pages of this book, you'll realise that Adult ADHD isn't just about struggling to stay organised or maintain focus – it's about embracing the quirks and eccentricities that make life infinitely more colourful.

It's about finding humour in the midst of chaos and learning to laugh at the absurdity of it all.

So, whether you're someone navigating the maze of Adult ADHD yourself or simply curious about the delightful adventures it entails, sit back, relax, and prepare to be entertained. Because in these pages, you'll discover that when life gives you ADHD, you don't just make lemonade – you make a sparkling, fizzy concoction with a twist of humour and a sprinkle of joy.

Get ready to laugh, nod knowingly, and perhaps even shed a tear (though likely from laughter-induced eye-watering).

Welcome to the wonderfully wacky world of Adult ADHD – where every moment is an adventure, and every story is a gem waiting to be unearthed.

Enjoy the ride!

CHAPTER 1

Navigating Neurodiversity: A Personal and Professional Journey

By Bernadette Ashton

Hello, I'm Bernadette; it's my honour to work as an ADHD Coach with adults who have been diagnosed with ADHD or are pursuing an ADHD diagnosis. My role extends beyond that—I also specialise in delivering ADHD training courses to share valuable insights and knowledge.

I proudly hold the title of a Certified ADHD Life Coach and an Associate Certified Coach (ACC), and I wear that badge with the utmost enthusiasm and dedication. In 2011, I took the plunge and founded ADHD Lancashire. This vibrant community is a beacon of support for families and adults navigating their unique ADHD journeys. Our mission isn't just about understanding and embracing ADHD; it's also about advocating for acceptance and alleviating the feelings of isolation that often accompany this journey. Together, we're crafting a brighter path forward.

My journey in the world of ADHD started over 50 years ago as a child, although I was never aware of it until my adult years.

As I reflect on my childhood, a peculiar revelation dawns upon me. I unwittingly served as a prime source of dopamine for one of my mischievous brothers.

He had an uncanny knack for devising pranks that he found hilariously entertaining.

To make matters more interesting (or exasperating, depending on your perspective), my dear mother received several invitations from the school due to his pranks. I can still hear her recounting the teacher's assessment during one of her frequent visits: "When he's good, he's an absolute angel, but when he's bad, he's horrid and a true force of mischief." Ah, the tales of sibling dynamics!

When I started school, within a few months, my parents moved house, and I had to move to a different school. A move to a new school forced me to switch gears, and let me tell you, I was dead set against being in what we'd call the "reception class" today. Nope, I wanted to dive headfirst into the world of real learning, numbers, and writing. I was barely five, and some classmates in the next class were already on the brink of seven. They were reluctant to move me up a class. But I stood my ground, and eventually, they caved. I relished the challenge and powered through primary school.

Fast forward to age nine when I tackled the 11-plus exam. Even though I passed it, I was not allowed to move on to grammar school, so I had to revisit the final year at primary school again. Once I finally made it to the hallowed halls of the Grammar school, I discovered I was great at subjects like math, science, art, and anything hands-on, like woodworking and metalworking. But oh, English and subjects that demanded an excessive amount of writing? Not my cup of tea. I became a serial requester of class changes, seeking refuge in the subjects that truly stimulated my interest.

I also recall a handful of us yearning to master shorthand and typing. Our grammar school didn't offer these skills, but the head teacher said they expected we would exceed the realms of being a secretary.

So we ventured to night school with the head teacher's consent. Shorthand? I could handle it. Typing without a gazillion errors? Now, that was a challenge. Dyslexia never got mentioned during my education, and I don't recall it being on anyone else's radar either. Ah, the mysteries of yesteryears!

Much like ADHD, the tapestry of dyslexia weaves through my family's history, touching not only myself but also my mother, brother, and my son. Alongside the familiar challenges of processing information, remembering details, and the elusive hunt for words (anomia), I have vivid memories of my mother casually tossing random words into her conversations. When I'd point out these linguistic curveballs, she'd simply shrug and say, "You get what I mean, right?"

Now, let's fast-track to the year 2000, the year my son made his grand entrance into the world. He was an absolute bundle of joy, perpetually sporting a wide grin and radiating contentment—until he discovered his feet, that is. Unlike my two daughters, who took their time, with my eldest starting to toddle around 14 months and my second daughter at about 12 months, my son was on a mission. By the tender age of 10 months, he was already diligently pulling himself up and navigating the furniture. Remarkably, he was walking unassisted by the time he hit 11 months.

Once he realised the power of his little legs, trying to get him into a pram, a car seat, or simply holding him became an Olympic-level challenge.

He was also an avid sprinter, seizing any opportunity to dash off like a little whirlwind.

Before he even hit the ripe old age of two, our friends and family had bestowed upon him the name "Forrest," reminiscent of the famous "Forrest Gump."

Whenever we ventured to the park, it was as though he had discovered the essence of freedom itself. He refused to put on the brakes, dashing off with boundless energy. Fortunately, my strategy was to take him to vast, open spaces where he could run to his heart's content. On the flip side, bringing him along for a shopping excursion or social gatherings proved significantly more demanding if he had the urge to run.

Growing up surrounded by nothing but brothers and then having two daughters as my first children, I naturally assumed that my son was following my siblings' fine tradition. He was basically a carbon copy of my brother. All boys were genetically wired to be more physically active and more boisterous than girls.

It wasn't until he embarked on his school journey that the puzzle pieces began to fall into place. It became increasingly evident that his boundless energy and restlessness were more than just a case of being constantly on the move. He struggled mightily with the constraints and conformity demanded by the classroom setting. Before I knew it, the school's phone calls to schedule meetings or request his early pickup became a daily routine.

It was at these meetings I discovered my son was also having problems with availability for learning and struggling with reading. Which led to my son getting an SEN Statement and having a one-to-one teaching assistant.

His compulsion to make a quick getaway also became a regular feature. Initially, it was all about hiding away, whether in the confines of the school toilets or lurking behind the coats. But if an open door presented itself, he'd seize the opportunity and make a break for it like an escape artist.

Frequent cow encounters in the neighbouring farmer's field became common, thanks to my son's adventurous spirit. The teachers weren't exactly eager to venture into bovine territory after him. No, they would be on the phone to me to come and get him out of the field, which someday proved difficult as I worked 40 miles away a couple of days a week.

Yet, my son had a penchant for elevating his mischief to ever greater heights. Scaling the drainage pipe and staking out the school roof became his trademark moves. Just when we believed he had reached the zenith of his tree-climbing career, he stumbled upon a towering specimen that even had the local fire brigade on speed dial, equipped with a ladder that seemed to stretch as far as you could see.

As for his diagnoses, they read like a grocery list: ADHD, Autistic Traits, Dyslexia, speech, language difficulties and learning difficulties. The pièce de resistance came during his tenure at his second primary school when he executed a daring escape, sprinting out of the primary school doors and taking refuge in a colossal school bin. It took them ages to unearth him from that unconventional hiding place. After that escapade, they felt that keeping him safe within the school's confines was more difficult.

His school years were an exhilarating rollercoaster ride, full of meetings, school changes, and the never-ending preparation for the adult world.

Over the past seven years of his employment journey, he's hopped between jobs more often than his sisters and me combined. It's like he has a magnetic attraction to learning how to do as many different jobs as possible. He seamlessly transitions from one position to the next, and sometimes, he even makes a round trip back to his previous jobs just for fun.

You see, his work ethic is nothing short of impressive. He's a diligent employee by day, tackling his responsibilities with gusto. But when he returns home, it's like a whirlwind hit the front door. Off to the gym, then boxing, and he adds running to the mix on some days. He's a veritable bundle of energy, bursting through the door with that signature mischievous grin plastered across his face as he contemplates fresh ways to prank me. The antics never cease with this one!

Currently, he's in the throes of enrolling to become a Royal Marine, and I have zero doubts that he'll excel at it. And here's the kicker: he recently had the brilliant idea to run a full marathon as part of his training despite never attempting such a feat before. The result? He not only finished but snagged a spot in the illustrious top 25%. He's not just reaching for the stars; he's lapping them.

My son inspired me to kick-start a support group in Lancashire for parents going through the same ADHD and Autism journey as me. Let's face it: this journey can be as isolating as trying to find a unicorn in a haystack when you don't have fellow travellers.

In 2013, I met Dean, an adult diagnosed with ADHD. We decided to take it a step further and established support groups for the grown-ups embarking on their own wild rides of assessments and diagnoses for ADHD and Autism.

And guess what?

These groups are still going strong, meeting twice a month, whether through the wonders of Zoom or the classic face-to-face rendezvous at various Lancashire venues. It's like a support group party that just won't quit! We have met many amazing adults during the past 10 years, and we still see some regularly at our group meetings.

With a blend of real-life adventures and some official training, I've become quite an expert in of Neurodiversity, especially ADHD, Autism and Dyslexia. This vast reservoir of wisdom propelled me to train as a Certified ADHD Life Coach. And, to add a dash of prestige to my repertoire, I continued to achieve ACC (Associate Certified Coach) certification from the International Coaching Federation right after graduating. Through my private coaching service, I have unleashed my treasure trove of experiences and insights, delivering and training courses for adults, parents, and professionals.

I am truly blessed and deeply honoured to have crossed paths with many remarkable individuals on this extraordinary journey. From all the fantastic people I have met from all over the world attending conferences, the wonderful colleagues I have met during my training, to everyone sharing their stories in this book. It's a journey that has led me to a profound realisation: that there exists a narrative that simply had to be penned, stories waiting to be told. It's the tale of the triumphs and treasures concealed within the realm of Adult ADHD, a story often overshadowed by its challenges.

I have also connected with countless adults starting their ADHD journeys who stand at the inception of their own unique odyssey, feeling adrift or perhaps a little overwhelmed and confused.

My heart aches for those who may be just setting foot on the path as an adult, unaware of the incredible potential ahead.

And it's precisely for these people that I felt compelled to create this book, to craft a story of hope, resilience, and transformation.

I wanted to offer them a glimpse of the possibility that stretches before them like a boundless horizon.

To assure them that success is not only attainable but inevitable amidst the trials and tribulations.

Through the pages of this book, I aim to illuminate a path that leads not just to success but to self-discovery and personal growth.

It's a testament to the incredible individuals I've had the privilege of meeting, a tribute to their courage, and a reminder that within each of us lies the power to become the person we aspire to be.

CHAPTER 2

Life Is Not Where You Start...

By Peter Aldcroft-Colling

Life is not where you start or where you end up.

Children start out in life with unbridled curiosity; they have energy and a desire to learn about everything. I certainly did! I don't doubt that I was an absolute handful for my parents. For example, trying to ride a tricycle up a slide was a perfectly valid experimental activity for my 3-year-old curious mind, but my nursery did not think it was a good idea!

For me, my ADHD has been a lifetime journey with both good and bad experiences. Now, with the benefit of hindsight (a wonderful thing), I see the world differently. Slowly, inch by inch, the world is beginning to see me and others with my condition differently, too.

Our education system teaches to the mean, and anyone outside of that will be poorly provided for. If you think about it, it stands to reason that only the middle 50% get a tailored education, even if they are lucky.

At seven years old, coming from a leafy rural Lancashire village, I was the intelligent little boy with whom the village school of the 1970s was ill-equipped to cope. This was a time long before special needs or teaching assistants.

So, I was sent to a "Unit for Maladjusted Children" to mix with others rejected by the system.

My small school could not help me despite my intelligence and innate curiosity. This was partly due to ignorance – nobody had heard of ADHD then – but also because it lacked the resources. The report from the educational psychologists even stated that I needed to be stimulated more!

But a small village school with two years in a class did not have the resources and still fails to receive them. The non-statemented budget is still based on the number of free school meals, and even now, the school must find the first £6,000.

I spent two years in the Unit, barely receiving an education – making candles from paraffin wax and reading Dr. Seuss's books. After this, I was returned to my primary school's final year without any support.

The loss of that time denied me an education, but more importantly my place in the social system. These social skills are the bits that they don't teach you; you negotiate them with your peers, and if you are with other misfits, they can't teach you as they don't know either.

I moved to secondary school, and my parents fought hard to keep me out of the remedial class. After five years, with a lot of grit, determination, and a few awesome teachers who believed not in what they saw – chaos and disorganisation – but in the potential they saw in me, I had made some progress and came out of secondary school with passable grades.

I struggled during the sixth form as the little structure I had around me was withdrawn, and I was expected to plan my own time and resources for A levels.

Most 16-year-olds adjust, but not many with ADHD can.

I got onto a BTEC Diploma, then a computer-aided design course, and from there into a start-up company.

I made many social errors, from oversharing to over-emotionality, but along with the downsides, it also brought opportunities. I sang in a male voice choir in Yorkshire and even performed at a concert at the Royal Albert Hall!

I always took on too many activities, sometimes working late into the night, burning the candle at both ends. By the age of 30, I had maintained a steady career and, through part-time study, achieved a degree in computing and later a technical rank in the T.A.

Progress stalled again in 2001 when I was 37. My son was starting primary school and having problems sitting still and being attentive in class. More worryingly, his hyperactive behaviour was described as a danger to himself and others.

Observing my son's behaviour at home and in school reminded me of my childhood. I started looking into the condition and the similarities between his behaviour and mine. I know this is a common occurrence, and many parents get their diagnosis when their children are diagnosed with ADHD.

Around the same time, I was given rote and boring tasks at work and struggled to stay on track with the assignments. Things went badly at work, and I was signed off for four weeks after breaking down under the pressure.

I sought a formal diagnosis, and at the time, the only route open to me was to go private. Work was very supportive and paid for me to have another set of IQ tests. The educational psychologist's report was passed on to my paediatric consultant, one of the few treating adult patients.

I was diagnosed in 2001. Since then, the world and I have come a long way. I graduated with an MSc from Oxford in 2006 and have gone from strength to strength, moving to an Information Assurance role in 2013.

It had been recognised in my childhood that I was intelligent, but my lack of self-belief had always held me back. It made me too defensive, as if I didn't believe in myself.

I had to prove to myself what I was capable of, so I finally took the MENSA IQ Test in 2019, and to my surprise, I passed. It wasn't whether I passed or failed; it was the knowing!

Having spent most of my life focusing on not failing rather than succeeding, external proof of my ability was necessary. I finally reached a point where I could believe in myself for the first time.

I had hidden in plain sight, along with many who have ADHD. By that, I mean being in a creative, ideas-based profession where you are expected to be interested in everything and where the artificial boundaries that the world places on your creativity matter less.

However, this had come at a cost. While I had managed to avoid the constant job changes experienced by some, my non-standard route and lack of inner confidence meant that I had failed to progress within my organisation. There comes a point where the sentiment is, 'By this stage in your career, you should have…'

I mentally gave up on career promotion and freed myself from the obligation to hide my differences at work. I posted a message on the internal company social media site, stating my experience and my belief that there were others in the organisation in my position.

From that, I started the ADHD support network in September 2021. I now lead a group of 50 'ADDers' within the organisation.

If I had one takeaway from my experiences, it would be this: You are what you decide you will be. So what if the world rejects you for being different? I recognise that my difference is a gift, and it is an important one.

The world rejects people because they are different. This is foolish, as it wastes some of the world's finest changemakers. Ideas and innovation come from those who are different. Art and inspiration come from those who are different.

The important thing is to believe in yourself and what you can be, not in the world that says you don't fit. We need a call not to arms but to ideas –to unleash the creativity and ability that lie within.

Now is the time! The world rapidly realises that with a population that is no longer growing (we have already peaked with the baby boom) and one that is quickly ageing and depopulating, we can no longer discard those who don't fit the norm, including the neurodiverse.

We need to broaden the definition of 'normal' to encompass more different people. One size does not fit all, and the damage done by telling people, 'You are a square peg, and you don't fit into a round hole,' is huge.

Instead, say to the child, 'You fit perfectly into the hole that is right for you, and if the world wants your skills and what you have to offer, then it needs to create a space for you.'

Much of the required change would be relatively inexpensive, as we currently group the 'able but different' in schools that tell them what they aren't. If we instead told them how capable they are and taught them in a manner that met their needs, they would learn more and become the creative powerhouses we need them to be.

We are not failures! We are not defective! Yet we are branded as if we are! The language we use to describe those who are neurodiverse is disabling. The same money, schools, and staff could be used to provide a different message to individuals whom the system currently excludes or places into special education. After all, if you are told you don't fit often enough, you come to believe it.

Fortunately, in the 21st century, we no longer need to rely on chalk and blackboards to transfer the teacher's notes to the student's notes; without engaging the minds of either of them .

We can and should use self-paced learning that allows everyone to progress at a speed appropriate for their level of mental development. As an August baby, I was nearly a year behind some of my peers in age, affecting my motor skills, yet this wasn't accounted for in my learning. Similarly, boys are disadvantaged by generally developing later and being less word-oriented. More is needed to accommodate these differences, too.

We could use learner profiling, as we sometimes do outside the formal education system.

This isn't just about the neurodiverse. We can create an environment where everyone can excel by teaching them at a pace and in a manner that suits them, not the system.

However, the lack of early engagement due to the poor provision of formal education disadvantages many socially, emotionally, and educationally. By the time a child is 7, it's often already too late.

It's time to shift the paradigm! It's time to change.

We can use more diverse ways to assess individuals' value and worth in the workplace. Most employees need to be more employed in relation to their abilities. Society chooses whether that's because individuals are better, worse, or different. Viewing it from the perspective of 'differently enabled' removes much of the damaging stigma.

After a lifetime of discomfort with myself, I am proud to be part of that change and believe in the power of embracing who I am rather than conforming to the world's expectations.

Life is not defined solely by where you start or where you end up. It's about the distance you travel and what you learn. The journey is what truly matters. As I turn 57, I reflect on the earlier parts of my life where I learned so much and seized countless opportunities. The crucial aspect was that I embraced the opportunities offered to me, even though those around me doubted my potential.

I stand on the threshold of the next 5-10 years, approaching the end of my career, the point where I can make a real difference. If you had asked me at any point in my life if I was successful, I would not have recognised the successes I have achieved. But I'm beginning to!

" *Having ADHD means having a brain in a constant dance party. It may be a bit chaotic, but it's always lively and full of surprises!*"

-Anonymous-

CHAPTER 3

To The Teen Who Struggles To Feel Accepted

By Rachael Beattie

To the teen who struggles with feeling accepted,

Hi, I'm Rachael; before learning can happen, you must believe you can learn. Sadly, many children with ADHD don't. If they have experienced failures, they can develop a fixed mindset and think, *"What's the point? I'll never succeed".*

Since I was five and told to go to school, I didn't want to go. I don't understand why I didn't want to attend school. But I just knew I didn't want to go. Was it because I didn't realise what they were trying to teach me? Because I didn't know how to connect and make friends? Or was it too overwhelming?

I just knew that I didn't want to go to school. I remember the days when I used to cry and cry to my mam, saying: "I just don't want to go mam".

"But you have to go to school," she replied.

I used to think, *why do I have to?*

My mam used to say: "this is where you have your learning", "this is where you connect and make friends", "this is where you grow and learn."

Another day, at the age of thirteen, I remember vividly. Another day of thinking, *I've got to get the bus, I've got to be on time, I've got to get dressed. I've got to interact and talk to people.*

I don't want to!

I still need help in the classroom, not understanding what the teacher has been discussing.

And that's when I'd go to school.

I'd been missing a lot of school during that time because I didn't like being there.

I still don't know why I didn't want to be there. Yet again, it's probably because I didn't feel like I fit in anywhere.

I'll take you on some adventure back when I was about fourteen. I started to drink on the weekends in the park. Then it went into going out at night. Still only fourteen years old!

However, I loved being part of a world where everyone was going out. They were older. They were around nineteen years old, and I had become one of them.

I was part of this world where I could go out, get in cars with boys, get dressed up, wear makeup, sneak out, and pretend that I was sleeping at my friend's house. Instead, I started going out with these older people to pubs. I am only fourteen or fifteen years old, but honestly, it unlocked something inside of me at the time.

I would save my dinner money. I wouldn't even eat throughout the week so I could keep my money to buy drinks, tabs and bus fare.

I would sell my granny to get myself out on a weekend. It was all I lived for. I lived for the fast weekends, the highs, the blowout music, the getting dressed up, the sneaking about, the connecting with boys via texts - It was so exciting.-

My brain felt happy. Extremely happy.

I was using this alcohol as a confidence boost. This was my thing. It made me feel like I was unstoppable. I felt like I could dance. I could laugh, I could sing, and I could be happy. Different. Happy.

Then, at about sixteen years old, I thought, *"Right, that's it!"*

I'm not going to school anymore.

So I left school with no GCSEs. I left school thinking I was a failure and couldn't do what I was told I should be doing at that age.

But I decided that I wanted to be in this grown-up world, so I went and started to be in the adult world of college. So, I took myself to our local college; I knew this would be the start of building my qualifications. Having no GCSEs, I started at the lower level of ICT, but before I knew it, I was moved by my tutor to the advanced studies, which had never happened to me before! College was the place that helped me to grow. But I was still living for the weekends, using alcohol to be that boost of confidence.

However, before long, that turned into Wednesday night, Thursday night, and Friday night, as well as the weekend, and using alcohol to get through the days and focus on something exciting.-

I realise now that my brain needs that excitement to feel happy.-

So, what does that mean?

Now, at an older age and being diagnosed with ADHD, I know that my brain needs stimulation to be happy.

I know that stimulation can come in many different forms. Now, I can understand more and find the right coping strategies.-

Things like going to the gym, walking, or running. These were the things that I used to help recover from my alcohol addiction. It was my new confidence boost.

My alcohol at the time was the thing that I used to let me talk to people, understand, and let my brain do its thing. But now, being older, I no longer use alcohol to change my mood.

It's great to be able to say that. It's such a proud moment.

There were days when all that mattered was alcohol and food, things like sugar and binge eating.

The binge eating was out of control because when you eat chocolate and sugary things in this way, it hits your brain with dopamine.

I now know my brain needs lots of dopamine and serotonin to make me happy.

The things that help my confidence and coping are strategies like exercise, along with talking therapies, yoga, walking and cold-water therapy.

Walking the dogs, seeing friends, drinking coffee, dancing in the kitchen, and asking for help. It all helps!

Also, being diagnosed with ADHD.

This means I have a neurodivergent brain.

My brain is awesome. My brain is amazing.

My brain works amazingly now, but back when I was twelve years old, I thought I was sick and stupid. That I couldn't do it. I was broken.

But actually, we are unstoppable.

"Success is not final, failure is not fatal: It is the courage to continue that counts."

-Winston Churchill-

CHAPTER 4

How The Hell Did I Get Here?

By Jen Bee

When I agreed to write this chapter, I thought, "No problem! I've got ridiculous stories for days!." Apparently, I can only recall my funny, crazy, embarrassing, and inspiring tales during first dates or when making life-long Facebook friends in random public bathrooms. Where are they when I want to use my self-deprecating humour for good? Maybe I shouldn't have a specific story in mind. Asking me to make a long story short is like asking me to whisper—yeah, I'll try, but there's no guarantee.

While grappling with this writing challenge, I can't help but think back to all of my chance encounters with strangers, unexpected adventures and everything else I have done. It makes me wonder, "How did I get here?" Seriously, there's a part of me that believes I should've died years ago from some of the situations I've been in from my ADHD. Yet, another part of me thinks it's my ADHD that saved me from myself. One thing's for sure—I wouldn't be where I am today without it.

So, where exactly am I? To explain how I got here, I should let you know where here is.

Allow me to introduce myself. I'm Jen. I'm 45 years old and still figuring out what I want to be when I grow up. Over the past 25 years, I've been...*takes a deep breath*... a bartender, car dealer, art dealer, boat stew, store manager, graphic designer, gym rep, server, beer wench, realtor, bar owner, marketing director, website designer, marketing "CEO," and most recently, an ADHD coach. *Exhales* Phew! Oh, did I mention I live with my parents?

Now, I'm sure you've got some burning questions:

"What the hell?"

"What's with all the jobs?"

"Is CEO in quotes?"

"What DO you want to be when you grow up?"

Don't worry; I've got some answers for you.

What the hell?

My story starts at 15 when I was diagnosed with ADHD. Back then, there wasn't much information about it. All I knew was that it held me back from being the brilliant student I was supposed to be. You know the story—"smart but doesn't apply herself." I was even told I might not get into college, which is unacceptable in my family. In the second semester of 9th grade, I started taking Dexedrine, which made all the difference. Suddenly, I was eager to learn, excited about understanding things, and even managed to get into my dream school. Mission accomplished, no need for the drugs anymore; I got this!

"But Jen didn't have this." *Insert Morgan Freeman voice*

I was all over the place in college. Freedom hit me hard. I switched majors from architecture to art, leaving my meds behind because staying hyper-focused on art projects beats trying to grasp physics any day. Making out was even more fun than making art, and I was all about frat parties and boys.

When college costs became overwhelming, I took a two-year break, ventured into sales, and got entangled in a toxic relationship. When that didn't work out, I started bartending before returning to school with a renewed sense of purpose - to graduate!

What's with all the jobs?

Having proved to everyone (including myself) that I could finish college, I was now burdened with the task that almost broke me—getting a "real" job. That's the deal. Go to college, graduate, get a career, retire, die. I spent years trying to follow the script. I knew my parents didn't want a bartender for a daughter; they had higher expectations, like an architect or artist. My mom would say, "I didn't spend $80k for you to pour drinks!" Her words stuck with me. In my mind, if a job lacked a fancy title or benefits, it made me a disappointment and a failure. So I went from job to job, seeking one that would make my parents proud or earn me a ton of money (neither of which happened!). I also went from town to town, moving from Charlottesville, Virginia, to Key West, Florida, then to Tampa, Florida, and Washington, D.C., before heading to Seattle, Washington. A move every two years or so probably didn't help me career-wise, but why be an adult if you can't explore the world? I knew I'd figure out a way to make it work.

In Seattle, I landed a fast-paced job that gave me both a title and money, but it nearly killed me. My ADHD brain was working overtime to keep up with the chaos, yet I had been coping without meds for so long it didn't even occur to me that my struggles might be ADHD-related. Eventually, I hit a breaking point and quit. I travelled, ran away, and ended up in Central America for four years, where I followed Tim Gunn's advice and made it work. I got a job under the table in real estate marketing and bartended before finally starting my own marketing business.

Is CEO in quotes?

You know that feeling when you're good at something, but the minute you put yourself out there, you question your abilities? Cue the imposter syndrome! So yes, "CEO" is in quotes! No matter how well I was doing or how many clients I had, I felt like a fraud, as if I was "playing" a business owner. It's strange, right? I had the skills and knowledge, but I still questioned myself.

When I was younger, my mom saw me as quick-witted and hilarious (I still am!). She suggested I become a comedian or work in advertising. While I *was* voted Class Clown, a comedian wasn't in the cards. But as I questioned my path, I wondered why I chose marketing. My business was born out of necessity. I loved the creativity involved in branding and enjoyed a good challenge. But deep down, I wondered if this was my true passion.

Everything else had been a job. Everything else I could leave and bounce back. If I didn't make this work, I really would be a failure.

Just as I started to figure out my life, it threw a curveball—the pandemic hit. With some time to focus (as much as untreated ADHD allows), I tried to pivot my business into something I was genuinely passionate about, not just something at which I excelled. Around the same time, my mom needed surgery, which required me to move back to the States to help with her recovery. I took the opportunity to consult with a psychiatrist and get back on medication. It was as if I was taking them for the first time! The revelation hit me—I had spent 25 years attributing my quirks, hyper-fixations, outbursts, and upsets to my loud personality, not realizing how much my ADHD influenced my life. I mean, I was diagnosed at a young age and, at the time, under the impression that ADHD was just a schoolwork problem, not an all-encompassing, life-altering disability. But at this moment, as in school, I needed the extra push to stay on task and get shit done, so I turned to what had worked in the past.

Then, I shifted my focus to hospitality marketing, which seemed like a perfect fit. It aligned all my expertise and experiences. Finally, it felt like everything was falling into place, and it suddenly made sense— I made it make sense. Every skill that I learned in every random position I held was being used. The bartending, the sales, the design, and marketing... were all coming together. I was made for this role...or was I?

Something was still missing.

During my rebranding journey, a friend with ADHD was struggling to stay focused on her business and mentioned attending an ADHD conference. I had no idea such conferences existed! Then she introduced me to the concept of an ADHD coach—a completely new idea for me, but I was intrigued!

Initially, I intended to continue with my rebranded hospitality marketing business while exploring how ADHD coaching might help me get my life and business on the right track. But attending my first coaching class was a revelation—I felt different. As if a weight had lifted, and I no longer needed to pretend. That feeling of authenticity was what I had long longed for in my business. It made me realize why I felt like an imposter —it had nothing to do with my skills or knowledge but everything to do with how I perceived myself to get the business. My clients love my quirks and outside-the-box thinking when working with me, but that was a side I didn't get to show until after the contracts were signed. As an ADHD coach, I could finally embrace that side because my clients were like me. I didn't have to hide my true self anymore. I found my unique value proposition. This was what I was meant to do. This was my purpose and passion!

What DO you want to be when you grow up...?

And that brings us to where we are today. I'm still Jen, 45, still living with my parents, but now, I'm working as an ADHD coach, guiding others on their ADHD journeys. But my journey doesn't end here. At 45, I surprised even myself by deciding to go back to school. I'm studying for the Graduate Record Exam, and next fall, I plan to embark on a doctorate. Now I know after that short trip you took on the Hot-Mess Express, you might think, "WHAAAA?" Trust me, no one is more shocked than I am. But guess what? Just because I didn't envision this path doesn't mean it's not where I'm meant to be.

No one imagines being 45 and living with their parents, and I know many people who never would. But you know what? It doesn't mean there's something wrong with me or that I've taken the wrong turn. My path hasn't been conventional, but then again, what is with ADHD? My ultimate goal is to help others find their path and embrace who they are so that they may live authentically. I hope someone reading this realizes that, despite the distractions and detours, it's okay; we'll eventually get there.

CHAPTER 5

From Mess to Success: The Bumpy Road to Reaching my Potential

By Alan P Brown

I'm an ADHD/Productivity Coach, which is kind of ironic. Because for most of my life, before I was diagnosed at age 36, I was the poster child for not getting things finished on time (it took me 10 years to get a 4-year degree), being irresponsible (I crashed every car I ever owned, plus two of my parents' and one girlfriend's father's) and not living to my potential in oh so many ways (I almost didn't graduate from high school, and my "gap year" – the year high school grads go out and explore the world before starting college – I pumped gas and bartended at a tavern).

Worse, in my twenties, I began self-medicating with alcohol and drugs, which didn't end well: I ended up a pretty bad drug addict.

But once I "hit bottom" (a story too dark for this uplifting book), I was able to climb out and get my first 'real job' as an ad exec in New York City…at the age of thirty…where my entry-level peers were eight years younger than me. (Luckily, I looked younger than my age.)

And at the time still being undiagnosed, my first six years were frustrating, with little progress "up the corporate ladder."

At one point early on, my boss was diagnosed with ADHD after his son was. So I went to my doctor on Manhattan's Upper East Side with my inquiry, to which he replied, and I quote, "Oh Alan, ADHD is a myth created by the media. You just need to do more crossword puzzles." This is from an M.D. in one of the wealthiest neighbourhoods in the nation. Wow!

I'll share in one of my stories how, six years later, I finally got the diagnosis, but the happy ending is that my struggles and later successes as an executive and entrepreneur led me to help others do the same, with coaching and an online "virtual coach" program called ADD Crusher™.

And today I'm proud to call myself a "mess to success entrepreneur" and an advocate for those millions of adults out there in the world who remain as yet undiagnosed.

Story 1: I'm Pursuing a Degree in Philosophy? Ruh-Roh.

Growing up near Newark, New Jersey, my mostly working-class friends all thought I was pretty smart. My father was a journalist, with both my brother and sister following in his footsteps; they had high hopes for my academic and professional success. (Sure enough, I'm the only one of my childhood buddies who went to college.)

And with so much encouragement and faith from my friends and family, I thought I could conquer the world! So I entered college as a "pre-Law" undergrad student, with philosophy as my chosen major. A great playground for my "big brain"!

All went well the first semester – a basic logic course, some English 101-type stuff. But then we quickly veered into the *truly* intellectual stuff: Aristotle, St. Augustine, Thomas Aquinas...

These guys made the Stoics look like a 4th grade debate team.

My brain just couldn't read – let alone understand – this stuff. I had zero study habits, having barely gotten through high school. So now I start getting D's. And F's. And I'm at risk of getting bounced from college.

But I had a secret weapon that would save me (at least for a while): Professor Bob.

Professor Bob was a great guy and we got along famously. He also liked to drink – at the local tavern, where…I was the bartender!

Most nights he'd stop by and have a few, with most of those few 'on the house'. We'd have a lot of laughs and he'd leave a nice tip. But the best tip of all was that he'd go *very* easy on my grades. He'd let me slip through with a C when I should have gotten a D or F or Incomplete.

So I took every philosophy class Professor Bob taught. And thanks to our little "arrangement" (of course, I'm not proud of this form of cheating and I don't endorse it), I was able to hang on for a few more semesters.

Then two things ended my pre-Law undergrad endeavor, along with any fantasy of becoming a lawyer. First, I'd taken all of Prof. Bob's classes. None left!

But most importantly, it was the good professor who finally sat me down and convinced me that my talents probably lay elsewhere. A dose of frankness that gave me permission to then pursue music, and finally, economics, in which I earned a Bachelor of Science. (I love numbers!)

And therein lies the happy ending: Although it took several years to figure it out, I finally found something I was pretty good at – numbers and statistics – and was able to put all my (limited) attention and focus into it.

As Dr. Ned Hallowell is fond of saying, "Stop doing things you're not good at!"

Story 2: My First Exposure to a Productivity Tool. At the Age of 31.

As I mentioned, I call myself a "mess to success entrepreneur." But besides the aforementioned booze and drugs, just how messy *was* I?

Well…

I remember one day, about two years into my career as a junior executive at a major New York City ad agency, I was in the company cafeteria and noticed a young account exec talking with an art director and in her hand was a pad of paper with a list of items on it, some of which were scratched off, and others that weren't.

"Huh," I thought. "What a great idea! All the things you need to do…instead of trying to remember them…you write them down.

This list is on a notepad so that when you fill up one sheet you can just flip over a page and have a new sheet…and then each time you complete a task you scratch it off, so that you can be reminded that you already did it!"

I remember thinking, "This gal is BRILLIANT! *She* is gonna *go* places!"

…That's right folks. I did not know what a to-do list was.

Nor did I know that you could keep things organised using a tabbed folder! Wait -- you mean I can keep all the notes and memos related to this one project in a folder labelled Project So-and-So. Which is different, from this other folder, labelled Project Such-and-Such!

Who knew?! Another revelation!

(And all kidding aside, this was in part due to my undiagnosed ADHD –plus some mild dyslexia and dysgraphia, hanging around in bars for years rather than study halls, and the related effects of 10 years of alcohol abuse and drug addiction.)

But even after I got these and other productivity fundamentals down and started getting some raises and my first promotion (after two long years), I still performed way below my potential because I didn't know any of the performance secrets that most super-productive, successful executives know.

In closing, I'll share a handful of things I figured out that helped me eventually go from lowly account exec to Vice President and Employee of the Year at the largest ad agency in the U.S.:

1. I began fuelling my brain with protein (e.g., no more buttered croissants and sugared coffee for breakfast, and instead an egg sandwich).

2. I identified my mentally strongest time of day (morning – as is the case for most humans), and did only my toughest tasks in those hours. I saved easier, miscellaneous stuff for later in the day.

3. I recognised that I work better in isolation. So before I earned my own office, I escaped my cubicle by working in empty conference rooms and even nearby coffee shops.

I hope these stories have given you a smile or a chuckle, a dash of hope, and a few new things to try on your journey toward *your* potential!

Creator of ADD Crusher™

CHAPTER 6

My ADHD Journey

By Alison Clink

Hello, I'm Alison, the CEO and founder of Dundee and Angus ADHD Support Group. Since it was founded in 2013, this organisation has stood as a steadfast pillar of support for families and individuals navigating the intricate pathways of ADHD assessments and assistance in Scotland. Fuelled by my personal experience and an unwavering determination, I embarked on a mission.

My journey began as a mother, driven by love and concern for my son, who was undergoing the complex diagnosis process for ADHD. Confronted with the challenges of this journey, I recognised the need for a support system – a haven where families could find guidance, understanding, and shared experiences. Thus, ADHD Dundee and Angus came into existence, initially starting as a support group for families of children diagnosed with ADHD.

Over time, my vision expanded beyond the initial support group. Today, the organisation has transformed into a comprehensive network that not only aids families but also embraces the broader spectrum of ADHD challenges.

From youth groups that provide a safe space for young minds to parents' training courses equipping caregivers with essential tools, our organisation has grown into a hub of knowledge and empowerment.

We are also excited to announce the launch of our second adult support group in Angus. Furthermore, we are gearing up for a special celebration in October 2023 as we mark our 10th anniversary. In addition to these milestones, I have also attained certification as an ADHD Coach, specialising in working with adults who have been diagnosed with ADHD or are in the process of seeking a diagnosis.

My journey is a powerful example of how personal experience, channelled into collective efforts, can create a profound impact. It started with a modest support group and has since grown into a multifaceted organisation dedicated to nurturing growth and fostering understanding. It inspires everyone who believes in transforming challenges into opportunities.

Let me introduce you to my son.

Amidst the lively atmosphere of a town perpetually abuzz with the exuberance of childhood, there was a young lad who shone like a beacon in the night. That was my son, Sam – a whirlwind of energy and mischief bundled into one. With an unstoppable zeal, he possessed a remarkable talent for turning the most ordinary moments into uproarious spectacles. Sam was, at his core, a whirlwind of excitement, a human force of nature capable of conjuring storms of laughter and chaos with just a spark of his boundless enthusiasm.

At the young age of 8, Sam's life took an extraordinary turn when he was diagnosed with ADHD – Attention Deficit Hyperactivity Disorder. However, what could have been viewed as a daunting label was merely the beginning of an exhilarating rollercoaster journey filled with unexpected moments of laughter and discovery, twisting and turning along the way.

During Sam's initial years in primary school, his boundless energy guided his antics, often leaving teachers and spectators equally astonished and entertained. During this period, the headmaster emerged as Sam's guardian angel, a symbol of understanding amid the whirlwind. The headmaster watched with admiration and amusement as Sam sprinted through the schoolyard like a rocket on a sugar high. A simple chuckle and a knowing nod were enough for the headmaster to acknowledge Sam's distinct form of enthusiasm.

As the years flowed by gracefully, Sam's mischievous adventures transformed from charming antics into legendary tales. He possessed a natural gift for turning ordinary moments into unforgettable memories. There was the memorable day when he unintentionally ignited a pair of motorbikes, an incident playfully labelled "accidental pyromania." Then came the legendary bathroom flooding episode at a posh restaurant, where Sam's routine visit unexpectedly became an impromptu reenactment of Noah's Ark. Each escapade contributed to the rich tapestry of Sam's life, solidifying his status as a living legend within his community.

Amidst the tumultuous whirlwind of Sam's youthful adventures, I remained his unwavering anchor, steadfastly guiding us through the storm. In the initial stages of Sam's ADHD diagnosis, I struggled with a lack of comprehension about ADHD.

It was during this time that Sandra, a superhero nurse from CAHMS (Child and Adolescent Mental Health Services), came to our aid with her wisdom and guidance. Her sage advice included the idea of initiating an ADHD support group, turning what could have been chaos into a clear and purposeful mission.

A decade ago, a remarkable event unfolded, uniting hearts in the spirit of unity and discovery. This gathering, a familial assembly, was orchestrated with a singular purpose – to bring together those who were navigating the intricate landscape of ADHD. To their immense joy and solace, a diverse assembly of parents converged, each carrying their tales of triumphs and trials in raising children touched by the whirlwind of ADHD. As they convened, an atmosphere of shared laughter and heartfelt storytelling enveloped them, weaving the threads of their experiences into a tapestry of understanding and camaraderie.

These parents, once strangers, soon discovered that their shared journey forged bonds stronger than any adversity they faced. In this haven, they established, the radiant energy of their children wasn't merely tolerated but wholeheartedly embraced. It became a sanctuary where the vibrant spirits of their kids could soar freely, their unique qualities were celebrated, and the challenges they encountered were met with empathy and support.

Over the years, this gathering grew into a thriving community, a close-knit family of warriors and advocates for ADHD awareness and understanding. Their shared experiences became a wellspring of knowledge and strength, and their unity transformed challenges into opportunities for growth, resilience, and boundless love.

Together, they embarked on a journey that transcended the confines of ADHD, forging a path toward acceptance, empowerment, and a brighter future for all.

And thus, the journey of the ADHD Support Squadron commenced. Fuelled by determination and a dash of wild determination, they established a youth group tailored for these whirlwind youngsters.

The group rapidly gained momentum, its popularity soaring like wildfire, demanding larger spaces and evolving into a spectacular three-night extravaganza. Within this kinetic realm, young members zoomed around, their energy bouncing off the walls like a turbo-charged pinball machine.

Then, as if summoned by a powerful bolt of lightning, a generous £10,000 award struck like thunder from Shire Pharmaceuticals. This prestigious recognition celebrated the group's extraordinary ability to adapt and accommodate the ever-growing crowd of families seeking support. With this substantial financial backing, a torrent of assistance poured forth from every direction – it was akin to confetti raining down at a jubilant parade as a procession of remarkable figures stepped forward to offer their invaluable expertise and support.

Among these luminaries were Professor David Coghill, the esteemed guru of ADHD knowledge; Andrea Bilbow OBE, the indefatigable commander of the ADHD advocacy army; Marko Ferek, the ingenious maverick known for groundbreaking ideas; Bill Colley, the steady and unwavering anchor amidst the storm of ADHD challenges, along with a multitude of other dedicated individuals.

This sudden surge of support transformed the group's mission into a collaborative symphony, with each contributor bringing their unique notes of wisdom and experience to the score.

It was a harmonious blend of minds, a fusion of expertise and dedication, all aimed at enhancing the lives of those touched by ADHD. Together, they forged a path toward understanding, empowerment, and a brighter future for countless families and individuals within the ADHD community.

Conferences became a realm akin to Hogwarts, where wizards and sorcerers of knowledge gathered to share their spells for taming the magical mayhem of ADHD. Amid this enchanting atmosphere, I found my place as the guiding light – the ADHD coach who had not only weathered the storm but also held the cherished map to navigate its twists and turns.

Within this mystical world of conferences, I donned my robes of wisdom and experience, ready to impart the secrets that could help others harness the unique powers of ADHD. Each gathering was an opportunity to exchange incantations of understanding and strategies for success, forging connections with fellow wizards and sorcerers on this extraordinary journey.

As I stood before these gatherings of eager minds, it was clear that I had become a trusted sage, a mentor to those seeking to unravel the mysteries of ADHD's magic. Together, we embarked on a quest to unlock the potential within the whirlwinds of our minds and to transform what some might see as chaos into spells of creativity, brilliance, and resilience.

Here's to Sam, the whirlwind who never failed to ignite storms of laughter and chaos, leaving behind a trail of cherished memories and boundless joy. In our town, ADHD transformed into the hero's cape, revealing the extraordinary potential within every whirlwind. Through the ups and downs of Sam's journey, we learned that there's a silver lining just waiting to be discovered within every whirlwind. (1489 Words)

CHAPTER 7

Like A Pantomime Horse, But Drunk

By Tony Coward

My name is Tony Coward. Somehow, my squiggly career path finally straightened out when I became an ADHD coach.

My biggest and almost lifelong frustration has been trying to work out the missing piece. (I wasn't diagnosed as having ADHD until I was 48.) People told me I was smart, so why did I struggle so much? I couldn't work it out. It felt like looking into a black hole. You can't 'see' something that's missing, but I could certainly sense it. No one put the school reports together. This was in the 80's. They were pretty awful. As a teenager, I burned a lot of brain fuel trying to make sense of things. The difficulties persisted into adulthood. My parents have always been very supportive but must have been frustrated at my inability to progress. Occasionally, they would give voice to their frustration.

My 'career', if you can call it that, has been varied and interesting. If I had to write a CV, and hopefully I will never need to, it would have to be either very long or I would have to invent a career path that makes it look like I'm a dependable and reliable kind of guy to hide the truth. I've driven a taxi, transported yachts across Europe, been a tractor driver, farmed sheep, run a market stall, loaded parcels, sold garden furniture, and delivered soft drinks to pubs, and that's the shortlist. That's without using a calendar and filling in the many blanks.

The idea that ADHD might be the missing piece came during a TV programme. Rory Bremner on BBC's Horizon (good luck finding a link on the net). Even though my son had an ADHD diagnosis, the penny hadn't dropped. So, at the age of 48, I had a diagnosis and a label, but this didn't mean that I was any closer to understanding what ADHD meant to me or understanding the missing pieces. Of course, I read a lot and surfed the web in pursuit of answers, but after a while, although I had learned a lot, I became disillusioned. Where was the stuff that would give me *my* answers? Some of the things I found were useful, but much of the information seemed to relate to the average ADHD adult. I've never been average, and I don't know anyone who is. Science says that if your feet are in the fridge and your head is in the oven, your temperature is average. It doesn't explain why your head feels like it's on fire.

A year later, and still frustrated, I booked an appointment with a counsellor specialising in ADHD. I needed my answers. She suggested that I should consider becoming an ADHD coach. I procrastinated, but at the same time, I thought, 'What If?'

Somewhere around this time, I asked Mum for all my old school reports and read them with new eyes for the first time. It was there all the time! The lack of focus and the disruptive behaviour initially, the surprising turnaround in the middle and the belated journey towards something approaching academic redemption. I paid a visit to my old boarding school and met my housemaster, who had been instrumental in giving me the ability to turn things around.

Six months later and shortly before the pandemic changed everyone's concept of time, I booked myself into ADHD coach training with ADDCA and got myself a coach. Lockdown V1.0 meant that I could shut myself away and study. What a learning journey! Finally, all the pieces started to fall into place. It had only taken 50 years!

So, now I'm an ADHD coach myself. I get to talk to other adults and work with them to uncover their missing pieces. It's tremendously rewarding and stimulating work. Finally, I think I can say I made it!

My first contact with Becka was shortly after my diagnosis in 2018 while I was trying to make contact with an adult support group on the Isle of Wight. Their Facebook page was unresponsive to my join request, and I asked another Facebook group if anyone knew what was happening. It was Becka who responded.

Sometimes, I wonder what would have happened if she hadn't responded because so much that has happened since can be traced back to that. It's been life-changing.

Long story short, there was no active support group at that time. Becka and I exchanged more messages. We met. There was tea. We decided to start an adult ADHD support group. We made it happen. It led to friendships with some truly remarkable and inspirational people.

Eventually, my squiggly career path ran into yet another patch of quicksand, and I decided to train as an ADHD coach.

Becka decided to move to Scotland in 2020. At the time, I was transporting yachts, cars, and other things by trailer around the UK and Europe. Could I help move her and all her stuff? Well, of course, no brainer, I said 'yes'. I didn't need to think about the practicalities. It was some way off. I didn't at that time think it prudent to inform my wife. Later, this led to over-promised, over-committed, no-way-out moments.

As the day of departure came closer, I started to wrestle with how I would explain to my wife that I was planning a two-day road trip with another woman. There was no way out. It wasn't going to be pretty. How could I have been so stupid?

Two days before we left, my wife suffered a 'total sense of humour failure' when I casually dropped into a conversation about my forthcoming trip with Becka. A two-day road trip with another woman? How could I possibly think that she would be 'cool' with that?

I didn't make things easier, either. I don't let people down, so she was incandescent when I told her I would be going anyway. This, by the way, is not a lesson from the successful relationships playbook, in case you were wondering. This is exactly how not to do it.

We loaded Becka's furniture into a sheep trailer. Boxes, bags of clothes, her 11-year-old son, her cat, her elderly dog, Becka and I all squeezed into my 4x4 for the 400-mile drive North. The dog spent most of the journey snoring at both ends.

Me? Despite my wife's fury, I was thoroughly enjoying myself. I got to spend a couple of days with my bestie. We talked a lot on the way. Important stuff. Although I nearly returned to an empty house, it was a great trip.

PS. For a happy relationship, don't try this!

Annabel rang me one evening while I was in the kitchen trying to scare up supper. She was driving on the motorway and rang me to pass the time. She was on her way to meet a boyfriend. They had had a couple of dates, and she was on her way to his house for the first time. The car's Sat Nav was dealing with directions. All was well, and we chatted away for about 20 minutes while I chopped vegetables until Annabel realised that the Sat Nav was no longer working. Time for an

ADHD-style rescue! This meant opening Google Maps and working out where she was. She told me vaguely where the boyfriend lived, and I then made a route to guide her through the city to get her there. I could track her as she called out landmarks along the way, and I was her remote co-pilot. Although she got there in the end, it was two ADHD adults working with all the harmony of a pantomime horse where the back end is drunk. It's amazing how good we can be at muddling through when necessary.

Becka loved living in Scotland but had decided to return to the Isle of Wight. One evening, I was in her kitchen. My son, Tim, had come over. I'd picked him up, and on the way back, we had grabbed ourselves a takeaway from the local Chinese. I was sorting plates and takeaway boxes when Becka came in. After the 'hello, how are you?', Becka explained to Tim what she saw as my biggest ADHD impairment and my biggest strength.

"Your Dad is completely incapable of seeing washing up. It's as if it isn't there, like it doesn't exist, which is weird because everyone can see it. However, what amazes me about your Dad is that he looks to see what we need before he goes shopping and buys stuff before we've even run out! I can't work out how he does that!"

Before the time warp of the COVID pandemic, I provided specialist transport—mainly classic cars, yachts and equipment. Often, I travelled to Europe. One such job was to deliver an American school bus to a custom shop in Holland for restoration. The previous year, my best mate Ian and I had spent a few days together exploring World War 1 battlefields around the Somme and following the exploits of an ancestor of mine.

The bus delivery was a perfect opportunity to tack on a few days of battlefield stuff in Belgium. Like so many, he had an ancestor who had gone missing and about whom little was known. Just a name, a number and a regiment. This was a chance to find out more about him. His name was Francis Williams. He had died in the final few weeks of the war.

Once the bus was successfully delivered and I had another happy client, we headed towards Leper (Ypres), dropping the trailer at a storage facility on the way. The AirBnB we booked was a short walk from the Menin gate.

The following day, Ian was unwell. This was unusual as he would normally have stoically battered through whilst putting a brave face on it. So, I headed out alone on day one of our stay. I started with the large museum in town. Afterwards, I decided to drop in at a shop that sold WW1 stuff we had passed the day before. Luckily, it was a quiet day, and the owner very helpfully answered my questions. I wanted to know how missing soldiers had been found and how I could find out more about tracing what had been the last days of Francis Williams's life.

Armed with this knowledge, my ADHD 'gibbon' got to work. Now, I'm not one who hyperfocuses often (too easily distracted), but I was quickly sucked into a world of trench maps, battalion diaries and photographs of battlefields, destroyed buildings and mud. I hastily scribbled notes as I went, eager to find the next step that would take me closer to understanding what had happened. I should have been a detective! By the following morning, I had a timeline and tracked Francis Williams's movements three days before he died. I had the details of the action that had claimed his life. I also worked out the location where he had died within 50 yards.

This is what my ADHD 'gibbon' can achieve in hyperfocus mode.

The next day, Ian and I followed Francis Williams around the battlefield. I provided commentary as the tour guide. Later, I put together the information that the gibbon had found in a folder and sent it to Ian's parents, who wanted the information as part of the family history they were compiling.

Sometimes, ADHD brings moments of childlike glee. A parcel arrives from Amazon, say, and forgetting that you had ordered anything, your immediate response is, 'Ooh, a parcel for me, what could it be?' So, you start pulling open the packaging whilst trying to remember what, if anything, you might have ordered. Once open, there's that lovely moment of 'Oh yes! Now I remember!'

My son, Tim, and I had one of these moments on a family holiday in France. My daughter had finished her GCSEs, a cousin was getting married near Toulouse, and we hadn't holidayed as a family for quite some time. I decided to buy a motorhome, travel to the wedding, and tour France for a while. One lunchtime, I was getting myself organised in the little kitchen to boil something on the stove, and after half filling a saucepan with water, I accidentally knocked the pan against something. The sound was a cross between a Tibetan singing bowl, a gong and the sound you get in a cartoon when a character has done something stupid.

Tim's ears pricked up, so taking a wooden spoon, I tapped the pan again, and there it was again. We experimented by adding more water to the pan and seeing how the sound changed. Before long, we began filling other pans with water and tapping them. Each time savouring the acoustic beauty that we could create. Before long, the table had a variety of pans on it, and we were tapping the pans in turn and trying to work out how to create the perfect combination of sounds. We played like a pair of excited children for a while until my wife returned and told us to grow up. I never thought a saucepan, some water, and a wooden spoon would be the recipe for a perfect father/son bonding moment. Besides, I don't want to grow up; sometimes, I might want to play with spoons.

Hundreds of hours of coaching ADHD adults have led me to conclude that the fundamental question that ADHD poses isn't a question about ADHD at all. It is the question on which every individual life itself is built. Whether that individual is neuro 'spicy' or not, the struggle to find some answers may reach its zenith in the teenage years, although I've found that it revisits us from time to time as we become older. The question is simple - 'Who am I?'

Without a doubt, ADHD makes answering this question much more difficult. Often, when we begin to think we might be grasping some aspect of it and how it affects the way our brain works, we find that it slips away from us, like chasing a bar of soap around the bathtub.

I'll let you into a little secret if you think it's just you. It's everyone. But almost no one is trying as hard as you to work themselves out. And don't think for a moment that your average neurotypical has it all figured out, either. My 'research' would suggest that some of them haven't got a clue. There was a time when I doubted this, but then I read some dating profiles online and laughed myself back to sanity. There are some pretty delusional fruitcakes out there who don't seem to have a clue who they are or how to relate to other people.

At least you're asking the question and interested in finding some answers. So, give yourself some credit. Nobody else in the world truly knows how much sh*t you've waded through to get to where you are right now. Keep going; sometimes, it might not look or feel pretty, but you're doing your best. Keep going.

"The only way to do great work is to love what you do."

-Steve Jobs-

CHAPTER 8

Turning Tides: A Tale Of Addiction, ADHD And Transformative Coaching

By James Hansen

Hi, I'm James,

I am a specialist addictions counsellor and ADHD life coach. I provide 1-1 sessions either online or face-to-face. I assist others to navigate a better way of living. A father of 4 children, a husband, a friend and a business owner.

I grew up thinking and feeling like I didn't quite fit in with those around me. I felt different in certain environments and couldn't understand why. Flashback to my younger days, from the tender age of 11 to the somewhat questionable age of 23. In those formative years, I saw drugs and alcohol not just as substances but as companions. They were my go-to companions to quiet the internal storm inside my brain. Little did I know, I was unwittingly self-medicating to find a semblance of calm amidst the chaos.

In the wake of my son's diagnosis, a light bulb flashed above my head, revealing striking resemblances between his journey and my own. It was like looking through a mirror, and through it, I glimpsed a reflection that set me on a path of self-exploration. The idea that I might also have ADHD ignited a curiosity that couldn't be ignored.

It wasn't until the remarkable age of 37, after a remarkable 14-year voyage of recovery from the clutches of addiction, that the plot thickened. Amidst the triumph of overcoming addiction, another layer unfolded – an official ADHD diagnosis. It was as if I'd stumbled upon a secret passage in my mind, revealing a part of me that had long remained shrouded. It was at this point things started to make much more sense. As I navigated through the process of self-discovery and self-acceptance, I began to have a much healthier relationship with myself. I then saw a vision of hope that with the right help and support, I could start to manage my life much better.

By that juncture, I'd amassed over 17 years of specialised expertise in addiction. My role as an addiction counsellor had seen me navigate the turbulent waters of substance dependence. But life had more in store for me.

The stage expanded to encompass my new role as an ADHD Life coach. I've donned this hat with pride and passion for the past four years. My domain of proficiency now straddles two intricate landscapes where the threads of addiction and ADHD intertwine. My services include one-on-one interactions and intimate conversations where I share insights and guidance. These exchanges happen in face-to-face meetings or virtual platforms like Zoom, where distances are mere numbers. It doesn't stop there; I've opened the doors to knowledge-sharing by offering training sessions.

It's where the wisdom I've gleaned becomes a beacon for others. I've developed a 12-week "Escape the Chaos" program for those business owners with ADHD.

In the end, my story loops back to my son's diagnosis – the catalyst that sparked this journey of self-discovery and growth.

As I look ahead, I find myself standing at the crossroads of experience, expertise, and empathy, ready to illuminate the paths of those who tread similar journeys.

Learning felt like trying to catch smoke with a net in my younger days. It wasn't that the stuff they were teaching was as clear as mud; it was my brain doing the backstroke while everything else was doing the butterfly. Teachers must've thought I was auditioning for a role in a forgetfulness commercial because I couldn't seem to hang onto any information. They'd give me that look like, "Why is your brain playing hide-and-seek?"

In class, when things got as exciting as a wet blanket, I'd craft a pea shooter out of a pen. My targets? Everyone, including the teacher. My career as a classroom comedian wasn't met with a standing ovation. Little did I know that my knack for making people chuckle was connected to my ADHD.

Ah, memories! I once had this brilliant idea to channel my inner Tarzan and shimmy across a rope from a boat to the dock in East London. I was perched on a flimsy polystyrene box like it was a luxury cruise ship. Little did I realise I was dancing with danger and perilously close to a headline like "Adventurous Lad Takes Flight – Ends Up in Splashy Situation!"

Having grappled with addiction and relied on the company of drugs and alcohol from the tender age of 11 to 23, I had an epiphany that these substances had unknowingly become my way of coping with and treating a life with ADHD symptoms – a condition I knew nothing about until my eventual diagnosis.

The tumultuous experience of being thrust into homelessness at the fragile age of 15 was a bitter pill to swallow, accompanied by the heartache of parental rejection.

I was utterly oblivious to my role in this chaotic saga back then.

It wasn't until I found myself in a rehabilitation centre at the age of 20 that the fog began to lift, revealing the link between my youthful behaviour and the disintegration of my family ties. As the years rolled on and I celebrated 23 drug- and alcohol-free years, I embarked on a voyage of profound self-discovery and acceptance. This newfound perspective was amplified when I received my official ADHD diagnosis.

Armed with this knowledge, I dived into an educational journey to empower myself and extend a helping hand to my son. Through learning, I discovered how to navigate the intricate terrain of my mind and offer guidance to others on a similar path.

Oh, the charm of having a memory issue – I always knew I had one; I couldn't quite remember certain things, you know? I went to the memory clinic, and I've got to say I practically set a new record for forgetting appointments. It was like I was in a game of hide-and-seek with my schedule. Eventually, I bit the bullet and gave them a ring, confessing that seeing them was as elusive as finding a unicorn.

Their ingenious solution? Write the appointments down! But, of course, there was one tiny hitch: I couldn't recall where I'd tucked away the written evidence of my forgetfulness.

Now, in a glorious twist of fate, after my ADHD diagnosis, I've become a mastermind of organisation. I've concocted a system that does wonders for me and serves as a guiding light for countless others. I've got these to-do lists that are more practical and realistic.

I've even whipped up a morning and night routine.

My dietary choices? It's as balanced as a tightrope walker on a seesaw. And when it comes to tasks, I've got a buddy system – body doubling, they call it. It's like having a task accomplice, someone to nudge me back into focus. Connecting with folks? Oh, I'm practically the mayor of Social Ville. Balancing the fine art of home and work life? Let's say I've cracked that code with more finesse.

But wait, there's more! I'm diligent about my recovery, making sure that the shadow of cross-addiction knows better than to mess with me. Mindfulness is my trusty sidekick, taming my anxiety and giving my impulsiveness a run for its money. I've even turned walking into a Zen-like experience – call me the Mindful Walker. And to top it off, I've created a weekly structure that works for me.

For someone who could never see learning as a beautiful gift, not just for me but also for those I help. I embarked on a journey of learning. Topics of interest around addictions and ADHD. I studied at the University of Bath. Completing a 4-year foundation degree in addiction counselling & a Bachelor of Science degree in addiction counselling.

I left school with no GCSEs due to finding school so tough (it just wasn't set up. Completing this degree was a big deal. You see, I understand now that I pick things up more easily around topics of interest.

In 2015, I was presented with my degree from Kate Middleton (an actual princess). This was such a big achievement coming from active addiction living in a hostel in 1998. In 2011, I started to learn about the coexisting disorders that run alongside my ADHD.

I understand if I'm not managing my ADHD symptoms, I run the risk of being caught up in addictive, habitual behaviours, anxiety feelings, feeling low moods and on occasion experiencing bouts of depression, low self-esteem, and, let's not forget, experiencing rejection sensitivity dysphoria.

I understand my ADHD will not disappear. However, I can put things in place to help me manage my life much better. I will always have limitations; I no longer see this as a negative. This is me, and it's so beautiful to know that I'm not going to get everything right all the time. I know I am unique in my way. This is what makes me me.

I understand that we with ADHD have some fantastic qualities within the midst of our limitations. I can walk into a room and sense the low atmosphere. I have the gift of changing this with my amazing energy and wonderful sense of humour. I wouldn't do this at a funeral, right? Lol.

If you are feeling lost in your life right now, please reach out and ask for help. Gaining the right support from the right person is also important to understand. Keep knocking on them doors; eventually, they will open to the right support.

Let that inner child out and know it's ok to do so. I regularly push a trolley down the shopping isles and get on it for a ride. Enjoy your life, and fill it with happy memories.

This started more when I got my ADHD diagnosis. I began to understand that my authentic self was unique despite my limitations. Self-compassion is one of my top priorities in my life.

Thank you all for taking the time to read this chapter in this wonderful book.

CHAPTER 9

Difference In The Making

By Jan Hanson

In my head, when writing this chapter, I have been witty, sophisticated and focused, but when I put pen to paper, it is a very different story. All this whilst trying to microwave McGee's dinner (he is my assistance dog), stopping the spaghetti from boiling over, remembering if I have locked the gate properly and ordering McGee's food!

I am Jan, 58, a recently diagnosed with ADHD. I was one of those children who tried to fit in and not to be singled out, but you do not do yourself any favours when you choose woodwork and technical drawing as your options at secondary school when you are the only girl. I liked woodwork, and I did not understand that just because I was a girl, I had to do cooking and needlework like all the others. I could not cook anyway. I even managed to get crispy cakes wrong; they fell apart because they were too dry because I read the recipe wrong.

The one thing I was good at was swimming, which I did all the time, and by all the time, I mean four times a day, seven days a week. This was my world, and I loved it; you could say I was obsessed.

It was great; I could eat anything I wanted and only put on weight once I gave up swimming after I finished school and went to college.

I failed all my O-levels because I could not recall the required information when put under exam conditions. I can describe it as opening my head, taking out my brain before the exams, and collecting it again when I came out.

Story 1

Therefore, college was the backup plan; trying to conform as a secretarial student could have gone better - who thought a series of lines, dashes, and dots, then doing them darker, would transcribe to a language?

I had as much success with Pitman's Shorthand as I did with French and German. I somehow managed to learn to touch type, which some 42 years later, I can still do; maybe it was the patterns, perhaps the logic - who knows. I know everything else frustrated me. Who makes the leap from secretarial college to lifeguard at Pontins? That would be me - I was called eccentric, and that was at the tender age of 18. The questions were: why are you leaving home? Why do you want to swim? Why do you want to teach children to swim?

My answer was that I was passionate about what I did and was good at it, so why not? Little did I know I would leave home and never go back again. Of course, I knew I could wing it, but should I not have been thinking about stability and the fact I needed a new job? No, I signed up for a childcare qualification instead, but I had nowhere to live. I did find somewhere, but I also tried to prove I was better than everyone else and should be on the course, so I took on more study by doing more. While the rest of the group had one baby to study for two years, I studied twins!

Nursing came next; the best bit was practising injections by injecting oranges using them as target practice "180". It also worked when injecting people!

They did say my injections never hurt, so my technique must have been good; pity my darts playing was not the same!

I also got married while I was training; Mark was my stabling influence when I used to write to him when he was at uni. Yes, this was before mobile phones and texting; we had to send letters, and he had to rewrite my letters before he could read them and reply to them!

Story 2

A few years after I got married, we welcomed home my English Springer Spaniel Lynn, who had lived with my parents since I was 17. I had managed to convince them that she would have been destroyed if we had not given her a home. On the day we were due to collect her, an articulated lorry knocked me off my scooter, and I ended up in hospital, so my dad had to collect the dog; he was then bitten by her, which was not a good start. Once Lynn was at home, I promptly left home to start as a lifeguard at Pontins!

At this time, we lived near the sea, so we used to take Lynn onto the beach, where she liked to rescue stones from the sea and chase them along the beach. However, on one occasion, when my in-laws came to visit, and my father-in-law was walking behind me, I threw a stone for Lynn, and then he was holding his head as the stone I threw went backwards and hit him. I have since been banned from throwing anything because it could go anywhere; I have no control over where it will land or in which direction it could go.

My husband has often said the safest place is in front of me because the ball, frisbee or whatever I am throwing will never go forward. On numerous occasions, I have had a very confused dog looking for whatever I have thrown.

My family is everything to me, but I have often felt the odd one out when Mark and the boys have been telling jokes. I have never got what they have been talking about, or if I have, I am always one step behind, and by the time I have got what they said, they have moved on to something else; this includes all WhatsApp chats, resulting in some very hilarious mistimed replies from me.

My biggest hyperfocus and obsession has been studying, and it has lasted for 30 years! But it's all or nothing - I say I am not studying anymore to get things done. Get itchy feet as if something is missing, and sign up to do something else. At the moment, I am completing a Professional Doctorate in Education. I would say this stems from having to prove that the study methods I was trying to do at school were not the right ones for me. I am not a linear thinker but a holistic one, and I can see things from the big picture rather than individual components. Therefore, I find it difficult to visualise ideas if I cannot see them. It has invariably meant I have had to trust Mark's judgment when selecting items like my latest car, which I love.

Another obsession I have is stationery; Mark would say I have enough to open my shop! My son says, have you got this pen, notebook, or diary? Me, you can never have too many pens. What if you need to correct a mistake? It has got to be right.

Will I stop studying once I have got my doctorate? Ask me once I have got it! Due to the nature of my job, I would say no, as I am always doing continuous professional development to ensure that I can give my students and clients the best of me. For formal qualifications, I would have to say yes.

Story 3

I am forever losing things – the most recent has been my glasses! You would think, taking them off, putting them in the box, then putting them on again the next day. That is logical, and then add camping into the mix, plus shower blocks; now you can begin to see the picture. I also wear contact lenses; it was amusing that it took three days to realise that I had lost them, and that was when we got home and unpacked everything.

I have been self-employed for the last six years, working through agencies to assist neurodivergent and disabled students who receive the disabled students' allowances (DSA) to achieve their degrees, masters, or doctorates. I also work with clients awarded Access to Work (AtW). I deliver coaching, mentoring and assistive technology training. Having worked through the agencies, I am now embarking on this with my business, Difference in the Making. I am taking baby steps to ensure I give all my clients the quality and the best of me. The saying is true to ask a busy person to do more - currently, I am studying for my doctorate, which is now in the research phase, and training my owner-trained assistance dog, who is ten months old. He can only complete his training once he is at least 2 years old. My biggest problem is remembering all the instructions and not beating myself up not to fail him.

My uniqueness has given me strength, determination, passion, and drive to ensure I am me. What I mean by this is, at long last, I know who I am and like who I am. If you ever meet me, I have long silver and bright blue hair and wear dungarees, and I will not apologise for that because that is me. I will continue to have my good and bad days like everybody else, but now I recognise them, and I can say I am not working today, but I do not beat myself up about them anymore.

I will go for a long walk with my assistance dog McGee and get an extra cuddle.

CHAPTER 10

Late Diagnosed, With A Love For Life And Inspiring Others

By Jenny Haslam

Hi, I'm Jenny – a fun, adventure-seeking Neurodivergent woman who enjoys family time, travelling, helping others, taking on challenges and raising money for charity. This has even included a spot of fire walking!

I love being around people; however, the older I get, the more I want to be around the right kind of people... radiators, not drains. I'm at my best when helping others, planning something exciting, or/and solving problems... out-of-the-box thinking is what I do best.

Positivity is a huge part of my life, and I love nothing more than making people smile. I am also an advocate for self-care and mindfulness, which helps calm my racing thoughts. I'm happily married, with two amazing neurodivergent children, plus we have two dogs, three guinea pigs and two hamsters. I'm also the CEO of "Create Your Own Success" – a coaching business that I founded last year. Life is never dull! Just the way I like it.

In early 2020, just before my 40th birthday, I stumbled across an online article that changed my life. The subject was how ADHD showed up in women and girls.

I was eager to learn more, as part of my long-winded journey towards an ADHD assessment for my daughter.

I desperately wanted to know more about why things felt so difficult when it came to parenting.

It hadn't occurred to me that I might have ADHD myself, yet as I read the list of traits, I spotted a trend. I was mentally ticking all the boxes… impulsivity, overthinking, forgetfulness, poor sleep, disorganisation, emotional dysregulation, plus the many positives, including being empathetic, spontaneous, humorous, creative, kind and hardworking, to name a few. I had the biggest lightbulb moment and knew I had ADHD from reading the extensive list.

From that day, I hyper-focused on finding out as much as I possibly could. It became a double – no triple – mission… for me, my daughter, and my identical twin sister, who also had no idea until I shared my newfound knowledge. Now, we laugh at each other in the best possible way and find pure joy in being on this journey together.

After being turned away for a referral through my GP twice, I discovered the 'right to choose' pathway through even more research. Time passed, and in November 2021, I received a surprise text, which led me to complete two questionnaires. One month later, I had a 90-minute video assessment and received my ADHD diagnosis. The specialist said he knew within 5 minutes. It was an extraordinary feeling.

It took me one year to fully come to terms with my diagnosis, despite already knowing deep down.

I find this tricky to explain, but it's a different experience when a professional confirms your suspicions.

Despite some relief, my diagnosis brought new questions about my life, and I overanalysed almost everything – wondering what might have been if I had known that I had ADHD all those years ago.

Now I realise that everything I thought had happened to me, had really happened *for* me – it's all about perspective. I wouldn't be where I am now if my life had been different. Even the opportunity to contribute towards this book and bring hope to others is an honour and a personal achievement I am proud of.

I love to inspire others and have always wanted to write a book. Procrastination and the feeling of not being good enough used to hold me back! Then I did the inner work (coaching) to overcome this, and now I love helping others get past their blocks and limiting beliefs.

Despite my resistance towards diagnosis, I moved forward with the resilience and positivity that I had become accustomed to. I continued to wear the mask; however, something then changed. I'd gently been pushing myself towards true acceptance, and by January 2023, I was ready to embrace my ADHD. It is no coincidence that this was also the moment I decided to leave the corporate world, ready to become self-employed for good.

This time would be different because I was different. It was time to step into my authentic self and help others do the same. I now take great pride in saying that I LOVE my ADHD.

Despite the challenges, I know it's a gift and one that I get to share with the world. I also get to teach my children (my son is awaiting assessment) to embrace their gifts too.

Story 1

When it comes to ADHD-related stories, I have many! My working memory might be shocking, but my longer-term memory recall is pretty damn good.

Looking back on my somewhat chaotic life, I can see the funny side to my many mishaps. I'm not sure my mum (who sadly isn't here to ask) would agree, though, especially when I left the bath running, got distracted, and heard my mum shout, "There's water coming through the light fitting!". Whoops. We sat in the dark that entire night.

I also vividly remember when the passport office questioned me after losing my 3rd passport many years ago. As I went to pick up my replacement passport (I was flying to Spain the next day), I was quite literally given the Spanish Inquisition. I was told I would be formally interviewed if I lost my new passport. Curious as ever, I asked why. Their response? That I might have been selling passports on the black market. I don't think that guy appreciated my immediate laughter. To this day, I have no idea where my passports went, even after moving house a few times.

Another memory is a trip to London around 15 years ago. My husband was working in the city, and I spontaneously joined him. I had a fantastic day exploring and returned to the hotel without any hiccups. All I had to do was collect our bags and put them in the car. I did this, then handed the room key in at reception before returning to the car again.

Here comes the plot twist… I walked back, opened the boot, and found it empty!

I panicked, thinking our bags had been stolen. I looked around for help, and then the penny dropped.

Parked next to our car was the same model and colour. What were the chances? I quickly tapped on the other driver's window (he was just about to drive off) and asked him to open his boot. I wanted the ground to swallow me whole as I explained why.

While trying not to laugh, the man handed our bags over and went on his way. I got over my embarrassment and laughed so hard that the whole city could probably hear me. My husband returned moments later, and we laughed hysterically after I told him what had just happened.

The funny thing is that I've gone on to do similar things since then. As a family, we were shopping one day (a big mistake with children who get bored easily!), and my husband took the kids back to the car whilst I put everything in bags. In my own little world, with my thoughts in overdrive, I walked back to "our car". I opened the passenger door, got in, and then looked over to where my husband should have been, only to see a bemused man (not my husband) behind the wheel. I smiled, apologised, and got out of his car before turning around to see my family crying with laughter. I couldn't resist joining in. Even funnier, the car I got in wasn't the same as ours!

I've learned so much about myself (and others) since my ADHD diagnosis, and I know that so many hilarious memories were created because of this.

One of my biggest takeaways is to have as much fun as possible, embrace the chaos whilst also seeking some calm, and live with no regrets or self-criticism.

My life would be dull without ADHD, and I wouldn't have met some of the amazing people that are in my life because I finally learned how to be my neurodivergent self.

Story 2

Although it's been quite the ride, my life has changed for the better since getting my ADHD diagnosis, even when I was still accepting it.

After my 2nd redundancy, I was a woman on a mission and made some bold choices in early 2020. I woke myself up and knew my purpose was to help others live their best life. I excitedly joined an online group coaching programme and became a certified life coach 12 weeks later. I then started my own coaching business… feet first. I was nowhere near ready when I look back now. Subsequently, my first business failed, although the pandemic didn't help. Nothing went to plan that year, although it all worked out perfectly – I just didn't know this at the time.

However, I successfully created my own free Facebook group (The 'Create Your Own Happy' Hub) during the pandemic, and I still proudly run this today. For 4 years, I've helped women (with busy brains like me!) set bigger boundaries, learn how to stop putting themselves last, feel more confident, and ultimately know their worth. I am also a mental health first aider so there's a huge focus on emotional and mental wellbeing. New members are always welcome, and we are global!

I bounced back from my business flop and worked from home on a government-funded covid-recovery programme at the end of 2020. I trained, coached, and supported hundreds of people who lost their jobs during the pandemic.

This was so rewarding, especially the 1-2-1 coaching, where I was able to help many Neurodivergent individuals overcome individual barriers.

I took them from not feeling good enough and being unemployed, to starting a job they loved and knowing they were more than good enough.

This contract eventually ended, and I'd already made my mind up by January 2023… it was time to go it alone but properly this time. My company, "Create Your Own Success", was launched, and I haven't looked back. I get to help and inspire the most incredible people daily, and there is no better feeling than that.

From helping ADHD business owners learn how to strategize and experience real growth (without overwhelm), to powerful confidence & mindset coaching, I'm here making a difference. My signature group coaching experience "From Chaos to Calm in 66 Days" is perfect for busy brains, and some of the transformations have been incredible. This includes clients going from feeling chaotic and stressed, to feeling much calmer and happier… through asserting healthy boundaries and more self-care, without the guilt.

One of my superpowers is being able to see things from a different perspective in a non-judgmental way, and people find me easy to talk to. I love empowering people to make mindset shifts that help them create their success (or inner calm) in a way that's right for them. Each coaching experience is highly personalised.

I am confident that having ADHD has heavily contributed towards my own success and happiness, as the tough times have helped me to grow. Now, I feel extremely lucky to be in a position where I am helping others to grow.

Whereas some people might give up when times are hard, my unique brain has empowered me to bounce back, learn, see things in a positive way, be curious (and brave) enough to challenge the status quo, take risks, and live life to the full… on my terms. I no longer mask either, as I've found my tribe and wouldn't want life to be any other way. I am so thankful to be Neurodivergent, and I am here to be of service to others. Life doesn't get much better than this.

The positives of having ADHD, far outweighs the struggles. It really is all about perspective.

CHAPTER 11

My New Role As Me!

By Natasha Hickling

Hello, I'm Natasha!

People often say to me, 'Tell me something about yourself.' I can't count how many times I have been asked at interviews by doctors, by people I've met while travelling, by prospective new clients and potential new friends. Each and every time my head goes completely blank, it almost feels as if someone has stolen my brain and wants me to stand there looking like a rabbit in headlights.

I eventually found out, at age 27, what happens is the question is so big that my emotions suddenly rush in, and I become overwhelmed. My memories almost disappear, and I am suddenly lost for words. The emotional part of my brain, my Amygdala, takes over!

In contrast, if you ask me about my favourite country, musical, or marathon I am training for, my thoughts, memories, and words are centre stage, and I can talk for hours without even taking a breath. This is all down to what I now know as ADHD.

Like my life now, I will take this chapter one step at a time to remember the memories, the stories, and the journeys that have led me to where I am today without the emotions taking over too much. But I am human at the end of the day so that they may pop up occasionally!

I, Tasha Hickling, was diagnosed with ADHD at age 27. The Psychiatrist sat me down and told me he had diagnosed me with ADHD; he said, "So this is the beginning of your ADHD Journey". I burst out into laughter, much to his dismay... "nope, not at all," I replied, "I'm 27 years into it, and I finally have a name for the thing that's been a part of me all this time." Before the diagnosis, I just thought the things I did, felt and thought was "me being me". I was endlessly misdiagnosed, and they never quite added up. Then, ADHD, four letters were given to me, and two years later, a diagnosis of Autism, and boom. The light switches on.

What brought my attention to the light? The simple answer is that I have always known there was a switch and that I am different; I have an intense interest in life and endless energy. People think I always eat sugar and find simple things like washing up so dull that I will do anything to avoid them and forget anything that's unimportant or in my line of sight. After completing a degree in Musical Theatre, I decided to become a teacher; it lasted two years in the UK, and then I moved abroad to teach. I was living In China, bored and overwhelmed by my job and life in general, so I decided to add to my stress in less than 24 hours by applying for a Master's. As you do! Impulsivity: 1, Me: 0! During the research, I discovered what ADHD was, and it all seemed to go from there. Apart from the masters, that did not go anywhere apart from out of my life three months later.

My journey is like having spent my whole life in a play, but I didn't know my role and never quite met the director's and audience's expectations. Now I know I can finally play the part I was always meant to play: me! This play, my life, has gone through many shows, sequels, intervals, plot twists, adventures, knockbacks, and rewrites.

However, every scene has moments of hardships and dilemmas and moments of joy, laughter, love, connection, bright moments, and happy endings. It has to be entertaining to keep the ADHD mind engaged, after all.

After my diagnosis, a move back to the UK, and a change of careers, I am now 31, starring in my new role of Tasha, accepting all parts of me and making sense of it, mainly. I am now a Neurodivergent Life Coach; I help young adults, teens, and families find and navigate their unique roles in their theatre shows. After working with my ADHD coach, I know that helping people with their shows in an almost director role was my purpose and the next chapter of mine!

Let's get down to why we are here, the memories, the stories, and the quirks of being unique and having ADHD! I want to showcase the laughter, joy, and many hilarious moments my brain and being authentically me has given me. Like a coin, there are two sides, and the challenges with ADHD are complex, real, and can feel endless, but we also need to remember to validate and appreciate the other side. When I think about which stories to choose from, I mean there are hundreds; it's every day of my life. I chose the ones that shine out and those that I still keep with me to act as magic spotlights to help light the future ones.

My first memory has to be one of my most pivotal moments; I changed my life's direction in one evening. I will set the scene: one stormy cold evening in December 2015, and I was living in the UK. I was working as a teacher, and it was the end of a tough day. It was another day when I wondered if I had lost my brain or if it had just not woken up today. I had come to work, forgotten my bag, fell over, split my coat, and was late, and to top it off, it was raining good old England, not to mention it wasn't even 8 am yet.

The day got worse and worse as it went on. Exhausted at the end of the workday, I was scrambling with my stuff to get to my car when I screamed in the middle of the car park in the rain. I must have looked like a tiger being let loose out of a cage. I quickly got in my car, and one of my favourite songs came on…

"A Whole New World" from the film Aladdin. I just burst out laughing crying, and then it was almost as though everything else faded away, and the spotlight came on me, everything else in silhouette, and then a monologue. My internal monologue. "WHAT ARE YOU DOING? THIS IS NOT YOU. YOU ARE TASHA F*ING HICKLING!". At this moment, without a doubt or a second to even think, I rang my partner at the time and said… "Let's go, quit our jobs and travel like we have always wanted. Let's not wait. Let's do it now!". At first, I heard nothing; he didn't even question my weary, excitable, and crying tone; he replied: "I bloody love you, OK? When?". That was it. Three days later, we quit our jobs, and five months later, we left the UK for a world of adventure, interest, and wonder.

One of my favourite things about being Neurodivergent is the risk-taking and willingness to try new things, the innovation even in the most challenging times, the energy to take more steps, the determination, and the endless enjoyment of life!

We are butterflies, a show to be seen and learnt from, and hopefully follow in our footsteps. It didn't stop there. Six years of travelling and living in different countries, and to this day, if I am unhappy, I don't wait it out; I decide to write a new scene and get it off the ground. I only have one life, one play, so I must make the most of it!

The next act takes us to 2 years later, a trip to El Chaltén in Argentinian Patagonia. My partner at the time and I were booked for a 20 km hike. We were all excited; it had been planned for weeks, and we were raring to go. We arrived at the tiny town with a population of less than 1000 people, with joy, not knowing what to expect and our life in our suitcases. The night before we were at dinner, I suddenly had a realisation, what I call the aha moment. The moment in a film where you figure out who the killer is, all the pieces suddenly add up. We will be doing a 20 km hike tomorrow, with high altitude, snow, etc., and we have nothing prepared. No water bottle, hiking boots, food or lunch, or even clothes laid out. The panic inside me started to spill out. How on earth had we booked this extravagant hike without thinking about anything that mattered? To us, we had a bed to stay in and a map! After dinner, we researched the hike and found many websites stating how you needed to be well-prepared. They recommended being prepared in advance. In the small town, we found a shop that didn't sell much more than water and snacks. I have coeliac disease, so that made things a lot harder.

We settled for 2 litres of water, cereal bars, fruit and crisps. We did the hike and finished the 20 km, tired, exhausted, amazed, and laughing as we arrived back at the shop we started that morning, buying four more bottles of water, two bottles of coke, and just about as many crisps as we could carry!

These moments are when the excitement takes over, like stunts in a play; we focus on them and miss everything else happening! This was one of those moments when the important things we needed for the hike hadn't even come on the radar until it became urgent and last minute.

Now, when I book anything, I make it my mission to know exactly what I need and prepare most of the time! I have to say I don't think we have ever done a 20 km hike with 2 litres of water again, though. We live and learn like a dress rehearsal where you adjust for the next show ahead. As they say, the show must go on!

The last scene I would like to share takes place during the pandemic in 2020. I was in Malaysia at the time, had just been diagnosed with ADHD, and was trapped in our two-bedroom apartment (the health regulations at this time in Malaysia were that you weren't allowed to leave your apartment for a walk; this was for five weeks) on the 39th floor working and living with my partner Ben and our pets. So, as you can imagine and probably have also experienced, the hand of the villain of the ADHD mind, BOREDOM! Oh my, I was bored, and if I had to go on one more Zoom call or binge on one more Netflix series, I would seriously call this whole act off. I like to exaggerate a tad; I am an actress!

One morning, yet again on Instagram reels looking for stimulation, I had a sparkly and fascinating idea. I had been missing my running and was sad my half marathon meant to be held that day had been cancelled.

What if I did a marathon in this apartment?

My partner, family, and friends laughed and said how on earth?

But with an idea, that was it; I was locked in, no going back. Three weeks later, I did it, raised over £1000 for charity, had a focus, raised awareness for ADHD, and finally cured my boredom. I ran for 5 hours and 30 minutes and did 1032 laps around my apartment on the 39th floor.

Now, that was a considerable achievement, just like the others, a reflection of how much we can do when we use our talents, strengths, and quirks to our advantage. We can indeed be the hero, the saviour, and beat the villain in our story; we must write it and see where it takes us.

As I read over this chapter, as it's time to close, I think of how I look at these stories. A few years ago, I may have written these stories entirely differently; at the time, I saw my ADHD and life differently. I saw the negatives, the problems, and all the things that went wrong, like leaving a course until the last minute, a complex marathon process, and feeling so ashamed over not having anything prepared for my hike. When I share these stories, I see strength, courage, endless resilience, empathy, adventure, humour, and innovation, 100% me and my ADHD! Remember, it's the other side of the coin or the show's second act! We need to be able to turn it over to see it. You may not see it in your life now, but you will in time.

I leave you with this thought: The voyage to discovery is not seeking new landscapes but having new eyes.

You will find your way in the show that is your life, quirks and all; you need to be able to see it.

"In the end, we only regret the chances we didn't take."

-Lewis Carroll-

CHAPTER 12

Embracing My ADHD

By Beverley Nolker

Hello, I'm Beverley; receiving a late diagnosis of ADHD wasn't quite what I expected as I approached the grand old age of 48, however, it made a lot of sense of a confusing and somewhat hectic life. After my diagnosis, I remember watching a video about choreographer Gillian Lynne. It was part of a talk that the late, great Sir Ken Robinson gave. I was touched by Gillian Lynne's story. She had the support of her mother and a clever doctor who could see the spark inside Gillian that yearned to dance.

I may not be a world-class choreographer, but I have an innate ability to stand on the toes of anyone within a five-foot radius of where I am dancing. That aside, I shall offer some insight into my background.

I was the youngest in our family. The baby. The one who wasn't supposed to be here. Mum had been told, after bearing my sister, that she shouldn't have anymore. Five years later, however, I appeared. A lovely shade of blue with an umbilical cord wrapped around my neck.

I was inquisitive, commanding attention when I walked, ran or roly-polied into the room. I worried about everything and anything, sometimes dissolving into tears as I had built myself into a frenzy about something concerning me.

My parents were musicians, so the house was always full of a wonderful, eclectic mix of people. Evenings and weekends were a bountiful fusion of sounds and smell as my sister and I were whisked off to clubs and holiday parks whilst they performed.

I loved school. It was one of the most enjoyable times of my life. I remember, at primary school, my teacher, Mrs Mallow (I called her Mrs Marshmallow), used to send the children to me to get their spelling checked. I decided, at a young age, that I was going to be an 'Orthographist', a speller of words!

I was also a fidgeter. I couldn't sit still. Assemblies were the worst kind of torture. At a young age, I learned that meditation was the key to helping me cope.

I would sit cross-legged on the floor and imagine myself flying across all of the children sitting in the hall.

I even imagined myself jumping behind Mr Horsey (deputy head) while he stood on stage. Sometimes, I was so engrossed in my imaginary naughtiness that I didn't realise the assembly had finished and children were beginning to file out of the hall.

As I said earlier, I loved learning. However, finishing a task or staying on track was a problem.

Computers were confined to IBM headquarters and were not an everyday occurrence. We certainly did not have them at school. I would focus long enough to fill off a few paragraphs when tasked with writing an essay.

In the meantime, my brain was running away with itself, and I was struggling to put everything onto paper in any proper order. I would walk away from the task at hand and find something else to do. Cutting my Sindy doll's hair into a short, punk-style design or colouring it with marker pens was a common occurrence.

When I returned to my literary undertaking, I began to write and became quite perplexed that the handwriting wasn't exactly as it was in the previous paragraph. So, I'd start again, re-writing and re-writing until it was perfect.

The OCD in me, I suppose?

One of my teachers in my third year of secondary school (we were still a three-tier system) was perplexed by my erratic behaviour. So much so that she positioned me at a desk adjacent to hers so she could throw me a 'look' or bang the desk with her hand to command my attention whenever I was 'off with the fairies'. I vividly remember a parents' evening when my teacher met the full force of my mum. Mum and I had sat through six to seven minutes of a tirade containing as much criticism and negativity as my teacher could spew, culminating in 'You, madam, have a very precocious child!'

Mum stood up. I held my breath.

'That may be so.' Mum replied. 'But it's for me to say and not you!'

With that, she grabbed her purse and walked out. I sat there, eyes agog, looking at my teacher whilst listening to the 'clip-clop' of my mother's heels on the parquet floor.

It wasn't until I arrived home and dug out my dictionary that I realised my teacher had been paying me a compliment. Collin's English Dictionary defines precocious as;

"A precocious child is very <u>clever</u>, <u>mature</u>, or good at something, often in a way that you usually only <u>expect</u> to <u>find</u> in an <u>adult</u>."

In hindsight, I don't think Mum realised what it meant.

I, however, now did. I took it as a compliment and went to school, the next day, with a new found respect for my teacher.

My remaining years at primary school went by in a flash. I became one of the first prefects at our school, flew, regularly, across the stage, during lunch, with wings attached to my shoulders, singing Randy Crawford's, 'One Day I'll Fly Away' and had one of my literary efforts transformed into a play after winning a competition.

One of my more memorable yet forgettable memories was being instructed to draw a detailed diagram of a locust for the headmaster, as I'd forgotten to do my homework. I spent hours drawing, re-drawing the perfect locust, which he duly ripped up before my very eyes the next morning.

I loved school. Adored it, in fact. Hated, loathed and despised examinations. I froze during them. It was as if my brain had been sucked into a black hole vortex (is there such a thing?)

I managed to get the GCSE essentials but was stuck. What should I do with them? I had always wanted to teach, but career advice needed to be improved at my local Comprehensive School.

My best option was to stay in the sixth form and take 'business studies.' This consisted of Pitman shorthand, typing and commerce classes. I took to these new topics with fervour. I would take extra classes at lunchtime and after school.

I had now changed my career aspirations to become a Hansard writer in the Houses of Parliament. That was, however, until work experience week when I was shipped off to a local travel agency. I loved it.

Now, I want to be a travel agent! I qualified within two years whilst working on my days off for a television producer who offered me a job as his production assistant.

I wanted to be a production assistant! I trained with BBC Television and qualified within a short space of time.

I travelled throughout Europe, filming and editing sports events for a few years before travelling to California for two weeks of work and re-kindling romance with my childhood sweetheart, Dean. I returned to the UK and told my mother I was moving to the US of A to marry him.

Within three months, I had resigned from my job, sold my worldly goods (a car) and was winging my way to Albuquerque on a one-way ticket (impulsive much?!)

I married the love of my life six weeks later with a couple of Tasmanian Devils adorning the top of our wedding cake (they symbolised the tornado of energy I seemed to have).

In the space of four years, I worked as an office manager of a real estate office in Durango, Colorado, as an administrator in a travel school, as a banqueting manager in a hotel in Albuquerque, New Mexico and as an executive assistant to the president of an engineering firm in Los Angeles, California.

I had a positive mindset about everything. I applied for jobs I knew I could do but might not have the necessary qualifications (on paper) to guide me through the interview process. The Universe believed in me, too; my introvert/extrovert confidence helped as I usually managed to land the post!

We moved back to the UK, and I went back to TV production and re-energised my love of lifelong learning. I studied British

Sign Language in evening classes, and my tutor suggested I become a teacher. So I did!

My son was born in 2003. A beautiful bundle of love who screamed for the first 45 minutes 37 seconds of his life. (I didn't time it, we videoed it!)

It was apparent from an early age that there were issues he was going to contend with. Speech, language, and play therapists couldn't quite understand what might be holding him back. He was, to his family, perfect. Curious, inquisitive, clever, intelligent and mischievous. Primary school extolled their views until finally, he was diagnosed with ADHD at the age of eight. An educational psychologist added autism, dyslexia, social communication difficulties, aural processing disorder and anxiety at a later date.

When he was diagnosed, I was at a loss. I didn't know where to go to for advice. I remember attending an ADDISS conference in Canterbury, Kent and feeling like I was in the presence of 'my people.' Everything that I heard from the speakers made sense.

So, just over 13 years ago, our family began a journey. It did not require passports or foreign currency. It was more like understanding, knowledge, patience and collaboration on a whole new level.

In the beginning, we felt like a rabbit caught in the headlights. Not knowing which way to turn or where to start.

I started to read everything I could to help educate myself to help my son. I attended seminars and training courses and joined online forums to learn as much as possible. Eventually, I began an award-winning community support group, ADHD Sheppey, which is well-respected and attended week after week.

The children inspired me to write a short children's book, '*I Have Some Friends with ADHD*', which was illustrated by my friend and local artist, Richard Jefferies. It was inspired by the young neurodivergent people who struggle with friendships and to help other children understand that their differences make them the absolute best friends in the world.

I have since become a Certified ADHD and Executive Function Coach and am currently studying for a Masters' Degree in Autism and Neurodevelopmental Conditions. I am passionate about helping and supporting Neurodivergent people as they navigate the world around them.

We know that a plethora of impairments accompany ADHD, but if that is all we focus on, how can we move forward? I perceive my ADHD as a strength. I have overcome an enormous amount of adversity, but -

I am where I am ***because*** of ADHD.
I have achieved.
I have channelled my energy.
I am still aiming to move a few mountains!

ADHD has not changed me but has charged me with the energy to become a better version of myself, and I'm grateful for it.

"Hardships often prepare ordinary people for an extraordinary destiny."

-C.S. Lewis-

CHAPTER 13

Becoming Attentive

By Chris Maddocks

Hello, I'm Chris, a 30-year-old Process Operator employed at an Oil Refinery.

I was diagnosed with ADHD in early 2022. Before that, I had never considered the possibility of having ADHD. I had thought I had BPD or bipolar disorder because the doctors never thoroughly investigated my symptoms and simply prescribed antidepressants for my "anxiety" for years. I always knew it wasn't just "anxiety," I recognised that I was different, but I couldn't pinpoint what was wrong with me. I often wondered why I would lose my temper so quickly, why I was extremely impulsive and had difficulty understanding the value of money, why I was highly emotional, why I had a troubled relationship with alcohol and drugs, and why I despised criticism so much that even a minor comment like having a stain on my t-shirt would bother me for days.

It was an ex-girlfriend who suggested that I look into ADHD, which turned out to be the best thing she ever did for me. At first, I couldn't believe I had ADHD. I didn't fit the stereotypical image of a hyperactive and naughty person. I had done well in school, had a good job, and wasn't overly hyperactive. That's the misconception most people have about ADHD if they're not familiar with it. I couldn't have been more wrong.

As it turns out, I am hyperactive, but it's more of an internal restlessness. In the past, when talking to counsellors, I would often describe my brain as constantly active, never stopping. I now understand that I was unknowingly self-medicating with alcohol and drugs to cope with this restlessness.

Fortunately, I was able to get a private diagnosis because waiting lists and uncertainty didn't settle well with me (another ADHD trait I didn't realise I had). Once I received the diagnosis, I went through a grieving process, wondering how different my life could have been if I had been diagnosed earlier. If I had, some of the problems I faced might not have occurred, and I wouldn't have been plagued with so many unanswered questions about myself. However, since the diagnosis, I have found many answers and gained a sense of understanding. It has given me a foundation to start working on and learning new techniques to navigate my brain more effectively.

As I began to grasp how my ADHD brain functions, I felt the urge to raise awareness about the condition. So, I decided to start a clothing brand called Attentive. The purpose is to help neurodiverse individuals recognise and support each other and to encourage discussions about problems and conditions. Expressing your feelings can help calm your brain and make you feel less alone. The brand's logo is a small black-and-white brain, symbolising the black-and-white thinking that often comes with ADHD. Starting this brand has pushed me out of my comfort zone multiple times, and hearing other people's stories and connecting with them has made me feel less alone. It's like building a community that looks out for one another @attentive.apparel

Reckless Nights: Unveiling the Consequences of Impulsive Choices

During nights out with friends, I often got caught up in the moment and made impulsive decisions without considering the consequences. The combination of ADHD and impulsiveness led me to cross boundaries I shouldn't have.

Every night out, whether it was a quiet Tuesday or a big celebration, I wanted to be the life and soul of the party. I would go to great lengths to make each night unforgettable. Fuelled by copious amounts of alcohol and drugs, my impulsivity took control. I would order bottle after bottle of various drinks, disregarding any sense of moderation. I became the centre of attention, dancing on tables and initiating daring challenges. No one tried to stop me, and why would they? They were having a free night out! This behaviour continued for ten years, even after the clubs closed. I would sneak people back to my parent's house for a silent disco in my bedroom while they slept.

The next day, as the sun rose and birds chirped, I would still be awake, overwhelmed with regret and anxiety. I realised that my ADHD and impulsiveness had clouded my judgment again, leading me to engage in reckless behaviours every night out. When I say I'm all or nothing, having just one drink or taking it easy never crossed my mind.

I haven't consumed alcohol since October 2022. I realised that when I drink, I become a different person, trying to make people like me by buying things and acting out of character. In hindsight, I now understand that the "friends" I had when I was masking my insecurities and dealing with undiagnosed ADHD weren't my friends. I can now count on one hand the true friends I have. Giving up drinking and drugs was a more sobering experience than just abstaining from them.

Moral of the story:

Being true to yourself often means saying goodbye to certain people. It's a wake-up call when you realise who your true friends are and who has used you for their benefit.

The Castrol Kid: An Oil Mishap and a Lesson in Seeking Help

On a sunny afternoon in Ellesmere Port, about seven hours into my twelve-hour shift at work, I noticed the low oil light illuminating the van. Wanting to be proactive, despite my lack of knowledge about vehicles, I decided to top up the oil. Not having the correct oil and recalling others using turbine oil in the past, I parked near the oil shed and grabbed a 25-litre drum of Turbo 68. Lifted the bonnet, unscrewed the engine oil cap, and proceeded to "top up" the oil in the van. After a few minutes, I realised I had poured the entire drum into the engine, using the wrong oil and overfilling it with 25 litres. At that moment, I didn't realise my mistake and felt proud of myself for being proactive. I closed the bonnet, returned the oil drum, and entered the driver's seat. When I turned the key in the ignition, I heard a noise I had never heard before. The van wouldn't even start. Confused, I stepped out, scratched my head, and suddenly, the realisation of what I had done hit me. Worry and anxiety washed over me, and I thought, "Oh no, I'm going to get fired. I didn't mean to do this. I didn't know it was wrong."

I called for one of my colleagues on the radio to come and take a look, still not fully comprehending the situation. Several came over, lifted the bonnet, and witnessed oil pouring out of the dipstick like a volcanic eruption. One fell on the floor, laughing uncontrollably, while another attempted to start the van to no avail. The engine was seized entirely at that point. One of my colleagues searched for a spanner to undo the oil sump plug and began draining the engine oil, the 25 litres I had just put in. After draining the oil, we thought the van would start, but it remained seized. We tried pushing it, but the back wheels were locked. Nevertheless, at least it didn't look like someone had poured 25 litres of oil into the engine anymore.

Using a tow rope, we dragged the van, with its back wheels bouncing off the concrete, to a location where it wouldn't obstruct other vehicles on-site. From that day forward, I became known as the "Castrol Kid" at work. Surprisingly, the van got repaired, and someone is still driving it to this day!

Moral of the story:

Don't hesitate to ask for help if you're unsure about something. Even if you believe you're being proactive, it's important not to assume when unfamiliar with a task or situation.

A Tale of Mischief, Redemption, and Resourcefulness

I was quite a handful during my teenage years. However, at school, I managed to mask my behaviour exceptionally well. Due to my undiagnosed ADHD and poor impulse control, the police had been to my house multiple times after my mischievous escapades.

One day, things took a turn for the worse. I confronted someone down the road who attempted to steal sweets from Wendy's house in our backyard. Enraged, I decided to seek revenge. Knowing I couldn't beat him in a fight since he was much bigger than me, I devised a plan. I tied the fishing wire to a lamppost, intending to knock him off his bike as he rode by. However, my project went awry. As he rode through the wire at neck height, it snapped. Unsatisfied, I decided to take it a step further. I grabbed spare spray paint from repainting my BMX and covered the entire back of his fence.

A few hours later, the police showed up at my door. After speaking with them, I confessed to everything, feeling guilty and remorseful for my actions. Understandably, my parents were not pleased, and I received a grounding as punishment. They even cut off the power to my PlayStation 2. However, I still had access to the computer for homework, so I took matters into my own hands. I immediately went on YouTube and searched for a tutorial on rewiring a plug.

Finally, the day arrived when I felt ready. I asked my dad if I could have a spare plug, claiming it was for a science homework assignment. Although sceptical, my dad reluctantly handed over a spare plug, curious about what I was attempting to accomplish.

I carefully stripped the wires with steady hands, revealing the copper cores. I recalled the YouTube tutorial and connected the wires correctly, ensuring everything was secure. My heart raced as my dad plugged in the console and switched it on.

To my astonishment, the PlayStation sprang to life. The familiar startup sound echoed through the room, and my face lit up with pride and relief. I couldn't believe that I had successfully rewired the plug!

My dad, who had been silently observing, was amazed. He never expected his grounded son to fix the plug and demonstrate dedication and resourcefulness. My determination and newfound skills impressed him greatly, and witnessing my capabilities, he decided to lift my grounding. From that day forward, my dad allowed me to assist with various tasks around the house, realising that when I put my mind to something, I could achieve anything.

Moral of the story:

ADHD brings certain superpowers. Our ability to hyperfocus on something is exceptional, allowing us to think outside the box and absorb knowledge when interested in a subject. When you set your mind to it, there's nothing you can't achieve.

"What you get by achieving your goals is not as important as what you become by achieving your goals.."

-Zig Ziglar-

CHAPTER 14

My Journey With ADHD

By Steven McLaughlin

Hello, I'm Steven. In the quiet moments between thoughts, I often wondered if my mind resembled a bustling marketplace, with ideas and distractions clamouring for constant attention. This has been something that I have lived with now for fifty years.

My wife always knew there was something different about me, and one day, she presented me with an article on ADHD. While reading the article, it was like the penny had dropped, and I literally could have finished every sentence in the article. I realised my mind was not chaotic but rather a creative mind that looks at the world, challenges, and interactions differently, thanks to ADHD.

Growing up and until recently, I believed ADHD is something my family have and not me since I have always been successful in whatever I focus my attention on. This chapter is a glimpse into the intricate pathways and uncharted territories that have shaped my life.

Childhood classrooms were both sanctuaries and battlegrounds. While my classmates seemed to sit comfortably, I grappled with the constant urge to explore beyond the confines of textbooks and lectures.

Constantly being told by my teachers, "If only he paid more attention and applied himself, he could achieve so much more". The reality was I did not find school challenging. The monotonous ticking of the clock felt like a silent challenge—one that reminded me that my sense of time was as fluid as the thoughts flowing through my mind. About 18 months ago, my wife discovered my primary school reports, and this helped her understand why I was different, and she connected the dots to ADHD.

As I stepped into the corridors of secondary school, a new world of possibilities and challenges awaited me. Little did I know this period would become a battlefield where my mind's complexity would often clash with the rigid structure of academia. This resulted in attending three secondary schools in three different counties: Lincolnshire, London, and Kent.

At seventeen, having had various short-term employments, I decided to march to a different beat and joined the ranks of the armed forces (Royal Air Force). This decision was marked by both excitement and trepidation. The regimented lifestyle stood as a stark contrast to the dance of thoughts circulating in my mind. Meticulous attention to detail, adherence to routines, and swift response to orders were essential—yet they also posed as potential battlegrounds where my mind could both shine and falter.

Training drills demanded unwavering focus and adherence to instructions, which often conflicted with my mind's propensity for darting off in myriad directions. My external struggles were evident when trying to fit in alongside my internal struggles to maintain a structured mindset.

Due to a brush with alcohol at the age of sixteen, I took the personal decision not to drink alcohol and continued not drinking alcohol until my early thirties.

I believe it is for this reason that I successfully completed ten years in the armed forces.

Upon leaving the armed forces, once again, I had multiple short-term employments for around five years until I decided to step out and start my first financial services company, which I sold six years later, had a year out and then started another financial services company which I have been successfully running for over ten years.

My wife is my rock, and although we have only been together for ten years and married for five years, it puts a constant strain on our relationship when navigating the unique aspects of my ADHD. There were many times when my ADHD tested the waters of her patience. We discovered that the same traits that presented challenges also held hidden strengths. My wife believes communication will become our cornerstone— I need to understand how to build a bridge connecting my scattered thoughts to her patience and empathy. I learned that setting routines, using visual cues, and even laughing at my quirks were ways to turn challenges into opportunities for growth with the help of an experienced ADHD counsellor and accepting my formal diagnosis of attention deficit disorder and hyperactive disorder (ADHD).

Not thinking through consequences has always been an issue in my earlier years. I started with an uncle who thought it would be funny to keep tapping me with a toy hammer and not giving it back, so I went into another room, got a real hammer and hit his knee with it.

As a child, whilst living on an armed forces base, I was watching Blue Peter and decided to help with the milk bottle top challenge. I thought it was an excellent idea to head out on a Sunday morning and collect all milk bottle tops I could find.

This involved taking all the silver foil milk bottle tops off nearly 80 fresh milk bottles and arriving home to show my parents that I had collected these for the challenge. What I had not expected or considered was the number of parents arriving at my parents' house complaining that I had taken all their milk bottle tops and that my parents needed to replace all these bottles on a Sunday morning. I did not see the major issue, as they would throw these away anyway. Looking back, I can see this was early symptoms of my ADHD.

A further instance I can recall is never really fitting in, which now I understand can be a symptom of ADHD, and I was not invited to another child's party from the same school that I attended. I felt left out and did not understand why I had not been invited. Somehow, I got it into my head that it would be a good idea to run into his house, find the birthday cake and take a huge bite out of it, which I did. I had not thought through the consequences that subsequently followed.

I experience many periods of hyperfocus, where I become intensely engrossed in an activity. This can lead to unexpected scenarios. I recall one instance that started with a text message when organising our second date with my now-wife. The text message that began with "Your mission should you wish to accept this" led me to intensely research how to edit a video and build a website. In my mind, all I could think was how cool it would be to inject myself into the mission-impossible video that would start playing on a website as soon as I clicked the link.

This hyperfocus state allowed me to perfect the video on the website, and everything worked perfectly, and my creative streak shone through. However, I had not considered that my now-wife would need to answer all the questions correctly on the website to get the grid reference coordinates of where we needed to meet for our date.

On several occasions, influenced by more than one glass of wine, she kept ending up in the middle of the English Channel, which was not the expected meeting point. Thankfully, the next day, with a clear mind, she was able to gain the correct coordinates of the location for the date. People with ADHD tend to cut things fine, so on the morning of our date, I had a tyre blow out, needed to find a new tyre on a Sunday morning and arrived 90 minutes late.

It is known that people with ADHD sometimes have a compulsion to shop and impulse buy. On my wedding day, I was walking past a very exclusive jeweller, and they happened to have a second-hand Rolex watch, which I have desired for many years due to the six-year waiting list in the window for £42,000. Having tried it on, it took all my strength, and I was offered 0% finance on 50% of the price to walk away. The hardest part was telling my wife after we were married that I nearly bought that watch earlier in the day, not thinking about what the consequences might have been given that I was now married.

ADHD can provide many benefits, and all it takes sometimes is for someone to say something; then I am on it and considering all different scenarios, and before you know it, it is done and dusted. My wife came home in March and decided she was fed up commuting to London daily. We were watching a TV show called "A New Life in the Sun", and I said we don't have to be here. I can work from anywhere.

Before my wife knew it, I had booked flights for April to view properties in France and lined up 12 properties to view for April. I offered one, and the offer was accepted; I signed the initial paperwork in May, married in July, completed the property in October, and moved in November.

Unlocking Creativity:

ADHD has granted me a front-row seat to the theatre of unconventional ideas. My mind's ability to leap from one thought to another has paved the way for innovative solutions and creative breakthroughs, and I saw alternate business opportunities earlier than my peers. In the professional realm, this has translated into a knack for thinking outside the box, finding multiple approaches to problems, and breathing life into imaginative projects.

Hyperfocus as a Superpower:

While distractions abound, the gift of hyperfocus has often allowed me to dive deep into projects with unparalleled intensity. This superpower enables me to channel my attention into areas of passion or curiosity, leading to remarkably detailed and thorough outcomes. Harnessing this hyperfocus has propelled me to excel in tasks that demand intense concentration.

Adaptable Multitasking:

While multitasking is a skill many strive to master, ADHD has naturally allowed me to juggle tasks simultaneously. While this might seem chaotic to some, it enables me to respond swiftly to shifting priorities and manage various responsibilities. This adaptability has been an asset in both my professional and personal life.

Boundless Enthusiasm:

ADHD ignites a spark of enthusiasm that can light up even the most mundane tasks. This contagious energy can inspire colleagues, friends, and family, injecting a sense of vibrancy and excitement into shared experiences. It transforms challenges into adventures and routines into opportunities.

Seeing Patterns and Connections:

ADHD often invites me to see the world through a kaleidoscope of patterns and connections. This unique perspective aids in identifying underlying trends, uncovering relationships between seemingly unrelated elements and fostering a holistic understanding of complex subjects. This skill has proven invaluable in problem-solving and strategic thinking.

Resilience and Adaptability:

Navigating life with ADHD fosters a resilient spirit – an ability to weather storms, learn from setbacks, and emerge stronger. This resilience translates into adaptability, an essential trait in an ever-changing world. Whether professionally or personally, the capacity to pivot and thrive amidst challenges becomes second nature.

"Success is not the key to happiness. Happiness is the key to success. If you love what you are doing, you will be successful."

- Albert Schweitzer -

CHAPTER 15

Motivate The Mind

By Emily Nuttall

Hello, I am Emily. When I was young, growing up and starting to understand, navigate, explore, and connect with the world around me, I envisaged that my journey in life would be like all of the fairytales I used to have read to me. They made me believe that once I married my "prince charming," it would be my "happily ever after."

However, from the beginning when I arrived in this world until today, nearly at age 30, I would describe it in the words of Ronan Keating: "Life is a roller-coaster you just got to ride it." My mother has always told me that I have always been ambitious, daring, humorous, and a day-dreamer. Ambitious like an adventurer, daring like a dove, humorous like a hyena, and a day-dreamer, like I was always being and dreaming in my own fantasy world.

Unfortunately, so early on in my life, throughout my childhood, teens, and now into my late 20s and almost into my 30s, this wasn't the Emily that I was first known to be.

You see, I was a premature baby. My mother's waters broke at 24 weeks, and I arrived 8 weeks early, weighing only 4lbs 4oz. My first young ambitious adventure was the special care baby unit, until I was well enough to go to the baby ward and then be taken home.

As life continued on this adventure, I didn't start to meet all of the physical, intellectual, emotional, and social key milestones of other babies and young children like me, such as walking, talking, interacting with others, and the world around me.

So, after many tests, I was diagnosed with cerebral palsy at 12 months old. Cerebral palsy affects physical movement, development, and areas of intellectual development as a result of damage to the growth of the brain before, during, and just after birth, and other difficulties can then develop and present later on.

Growing up, I found it so hard to feel like I belonged in the world around me. To everyone else, I wasn't a "normal" baby, child, teenager, and later on, a young adult. I struggled to interpret and make sense of it all, almost like I was stuck in a washing machine on a constant spin cycle. This would lead me to having meltdowns, being angry, going off the rails, being disruptive, disengaging, often a distraction, being told I wasn't 'good enough,' that I was a constant mistake, a failure, impatient, and that I would never connect with my life, or others, or even the world around me.

I became a lost, broken, sad Emily, but I would just mask this with "I'm fine," which became my best friend. I would tell everyone that I was "fine" as, after all, that felt safer than being vulnerable, rejected, hurt, unloved, and unwanted.

Masking my life, trauma, pain, autism, and ADHD with "I'm fine" took me down a very scary 18-year pathway of battling depression, anger, meltdowns, fear, worry, anxiety, PTSD, self-harm, suicide attempts, and anorexia, with numerous inpatient and day patient admissions and ongoing outpatient therapy.

It led to me having to say yes to please everyone else, relationships breaking down, being unable to relax, self-punishment, hyperactivity, being afraid of forgetting everything, bottling up my feelings, darkness, and despair. It meant my overwhelm bucket was completely filling up and about to explode, which would then come out in extreme anger outbursts directed not only at myself but also at others around me. This would make me feel even more ashamed and more desperate for the mask to escape and the feelings of needing to turn to what felt like my best friends and comfort blankets of anorexia and self-harm. Having all these labels made me feel like I was not worthy of love, life, or being in this world. I felt like a pin-board of labels, hurt, pain, rejections, diagnoses, an un-organized mess, lazy, clumsy, and uncaring.

Another deep dark secret buried and internalised while all this was going on was that I had been hiding the emotional abuse and witnessing domestic violence that I had experienced throughout my childhood and teenage years by my ex-step-mother after my father had walked out of my life and re-married. She had taken great advantage, like Cinderella's step-mother, of these things about me, these labels and diagnoses. In "her" eyes, I would never be a normal or a wanted Emily. After all, she had framed me as worthless, useless, a burden, unlovable, and ugly for being different.

For 18 years, I let my life be controlled, impacted, and defined by the many physical, intellectual, emotional, and mental labels that cerebral palsy, autism, ADHD, anorexia, suicide, self-harm, depression, anxiety, abuse, and trauma had tried to impose on me. But now, I am truly starting to see in a new light that by being different, we succeed together. We learn from being unique and can become empowering role models for others.

I now embrace Emily with her differences, nurture younger Emily, and help present Emily to evolve in every possible way despite the pain and challenges. The saying "never be ashamed of your story; it will inspire others" has helped me become an expert by experience with local autism, learning disability, ADHD, mental health, social care, education, and eating disorder services. I aim to be a voice for those who don't feel heard so that they can rise above the clouds like me and become free. This is also helping me find my feet and independence by building and developing my new business venture called "Motivate The Mind," which will offer growth, learning, training, and development in all the life areas and challenges I have faced, with the hope of equipping our society to create a world where we are all heard, loved, worthy, enough, able to be understood, accepted, and to develop new projects, ideas, and support to grow each of us to our best abilities, united like an ADHD and life experience army.

ADHD, my struggles, and life experiences have nurtured the creative side within me. One of my great coping strategies has become poetry, storytelling, humour, magical memory, motivational music, and even what I humorously call "awful art." These elements, alongside my compassion, multitasking, evolving energy, ambition for life, acceptance of others, and my honesty motto, have been instrumental in helping me navigate life's challenges. Even in the most serious, traumatising, devastating, and painful situations, I make poems, art, and music out of everything in life. It's as if it helps me cope, providing a positive outlet for my emotions. Poetry, story-telling, humor, magical memory, motivational music and awful art is what I call my safe world.

My world where I am free, where I express the real Emily, it helps me to become free of labels, to allow my sense of humor to shine through, to feel present and connected and also be a positive way of coping.

I remember one day having to go for another assessment, this time for autism, ADHD, mental health, and an eating disorder. I had been assessed by multiple professionals in a matter of weeks. I walked into the room, took one look at the assessor with his big white beard, and blurted out, "Oh for god's sake, more paperwork that requires me to put more *beeping* ticks. You, sir, are an absolute *beep*." Looking back, I realise he cared and had my best interests at heart. His final words stayed with me: that no matter the outcome, these labels would never define me, and I would always be the best Emily I could be.

Even in the most challenging moments, I find hope in making poems, art, and music out of everything in life. These creative outlets allow me to express the real Emily, beyond the labels, and connect with others. There have been times when my humour got me into trouble, like the assessment incident. But these expressions give me hope in dark times, allowing me to express myself to myself and others. This helps people come into my mind and unique world, sit with me, and hold me on this journey, providing strength and hope that life and recovery are possible despite struggles.

Humour and making up unique and hilarious sayings in all kinds of situations helps me to also cope, then that is the best medicine. I often get told that I am the comedy clown. But it also gives me hope in the dark, lonely, and scary times. If I can't take my mask off, I can still express Emily to myself and others.

Removing this mask and showing the real Emily has been the scariest but bravest decision I have ever made as it allows people to hold me on this journey giving me strength and hope that life and recovery is truly possible.

Inside the darkness and all of my many struggles, trauma's, pains and challenges, I do have a purpose, that it is worth living and that can be one of the most beautiful things in the world to be able to show bravery, vulnerability and be empowered and show ADDmaration as Emily, because as Dear Evan Hansen reminds me and all of us from his famous song "you will be found" he holds us and tells us that " even when the dark comes crashing through, when you need a friend to carry you, when your lost and broken on the ground, you will be found".

In the end, I believe that ADHD, my struggles, and life experiences don't define me or anyone else. Instead, they allow our abilities, determination, hopes, and dreams to shine through. Success varies for each of us with similar life experiences and ADHD, and we should embrace it for ourselves. To those who doubted me, hurt me, and couldn't accept the Emily I am now in 2023, this is a reminder that I am brave, bruised, and I am who I am meant to be. ADHD and my life experiences are a story of hope for the world to see.

FEAR - Face Everything and Rise. When you face your struggles, you overcome them. The light at the end of the tunnel is always in sight, no matter how hard the battle. (1721 Words)

CHAPTER 16

ADHDtastic™: Crafting A Life That Aligns with my ADHD

By Kimberley B. Pereira

I'm Kim and I'm the founder of ADHD Coach CT. I am a mom of two, an entrepreneur, an experienced educator, and a lifelong learner, AND I have ADHD. While I am a late-diagnosed ADHDer, I always knew that I needed to do things differently to succeed. This never stopped me – I have been an educator for over 20 years and have a doctorate from Teachers College, Columbia University. Over the years, I've developed strategies and workarounds that enable me to minimise my ADHD-related challenges and to harness my greatest strengths.

I love learning (seriously, it's my primary core value and what led me to become an ADHD Coach), reading, traveling the world, and being active both physically and in my community.

While I currently reside in the United States, I was born in Canada and have also lived in England, Singapore and Argentina. As an ADHDer, I love exploring new places and trying new things (as long as it does not involve heights - as I am terrified of anything that requires being up high!).

Throughout my entire life, I knew that I experienced the world a little differently than others, but I never knew why.

For me, life was full of contradictions - why could I excel at school but constantly feel like an imposter in the real world even after obtaining my doctorate from an Ivy League school? Why was graduate school relatively easy for me when I was taking classes and certification exams, yet I felt overwhelmed and unsure how to proceed when I entered the dissertation phase? Why was it easy for me to plan travel or tackle a complicated problem that had others baffled, but I had no idea how to successfully execute a basic meal in the kitchen? Even more so, why did I have no interest in learning how to cook but I have a deep desire to learn so many other things?

Growing up in the 80s meant that I went to school at a time when society had a very narrow view of what ADHD looked like, and especially what it looked like in girls. Furthermore, my placement in the gifted and talented program in elementary school virtually ensured that I would never be evaluated for ADHD as a child, as the intersection between giftedness and ADHD was not really understood at the time. But as I look back on my childhood, there were so many signs and some of them seemed to be flashing in red saying, hello, she has ADHD! From constantly being told I had "verbal diarrhea", to my tendency to interrupt others (I was that kid in class with her hand up who desperately wanted to get the teachers attention as fast as possible before I forgot want I wanted to say), to my challenges reading social cues, the signs were there early on. But, it wasn't until my mid-40s when I started learning more about ADHD and what the research had discovered in the last few decades that I had my "aha" moment.

So, I flexed my ADHD hyperfocus strength and I went down the rabbit hole of learning everything I could about ADHD from books, research papers, podcasts, webinars and conferences.

All of a sudden, the puzzle pieces of my life that often appeared to not fit together all of a sudden began to make sense. I decided to see if my hunch was right and went through an extensive diagnosis process with a neuropsychologist and there it was in black and white - a formal diagnosis of ADHD. Whoa, now things started to make sense - all the contradictions, all the struggles and all the strategies I had unknowingly put into place to manage my symptoms. With my new ADHD "glasses" on, I could now see the futility of all the time I spent doing everything I could think of to try to belong and succeed in a neurotypical world.

Overall I was doing well as I had figured out how to mask and what strategies I needed to overcome some of my challenges, but the diagnosis gave me permission to admit that some things just are so much harder for me (and other things are just easier for me to do).

For example, I decided to stop beating myself up for my lack of culinary skills and finally just wave the white flag by admitting that I have no interest in cooking beyond doing what I need to do for survival.

Even more importantly, my ADHD diagnosis also gave me permission to show off my mad skills as an ADHDer in hyperfocus, and I continued down the rabbit hole of learning as much as possible about ADHD. So, what is an ADHDer to do but decide to impulsively pursue a new career path focused on

ADHD. Yes, the timeframe between when I decided to "just look into" what becoming an ADHD Coach involved to enrolling in an ADHD Coach training program was approximately one week - hello impulsivity!

Looking back, I wonder what may have happened if I hesitated (I expect that the program I enrolled in would have been full if I waited much longer so my journey would have taken much longer, or it may have been derailed), but I am so thankful my impulsivity took the reins and told me just to go for it.

The same hyperfocus and impulsivity kicked in when I decided to launch my ADHD Coaching business, ADHD Coach CT LLC. There is never a good time to start something new so I decided, what the hell, just go for it and it wasn't long until I got my first client and then more and more. Impulsivity - society views it as a negative but I argue that it CAN be a strength when channelled towards taking potentially positive risks. A common definition of impulsivity is the tendency to act without thinking, yet I think it can be spun positively as the willingness to take chances when something great can be possible. I actually think some of my worst decisions in life occurred when I started to second guess my instincts, listened to too many naysayers and took the path others wanted for me rather than the path I imagined or desired.

I want to be clear that being an adult with ADHD is not all rainbows and unicorns. I face challenges everyday with many of my executive functions. For example, I waited until the last minute to write this chapter as task initiation can be a struggle for me even though I've been involved in many large projects and even wrote a dissertation.

I can struggle with being inflexible and feeling overwhelmed when others change plans, but I love being the one to be spontaneous (as long as I am the one changing the plans). Emotional dysregulation is real and overwhelm is a physical sensation in my body that I can explicitly describe, not just an emotion I experience.

Now that I have an ADHD lens to view my past experiences through, all I can do is laugh at some of my reactions to events. For example, when I was a recent college graduate, I lived in a house with three roommates. It was Christmas time and my roommates wanted to get a live Christmas tree. I grew up with an artificial Christmas tree so the thought of having a live tree scared the living daylights out of me.

All I could think of were the stories I heard about house fires caused by Christmas trees that were not properly maintained, and I had no idea how to maintain a live tree. Rather than expressing those thoughts and feelings to my roommates, I decided that I was not going to be part of this crazy idea and refused to participate in the process of picking out the tree, setting it up or watering it (very mature of me, I know).

Seeing the Christmas tree everyday continued to overwhelm me, and I was not subtle about my disdain for this poor tree.

Yikes, in retrospect, I realise that I let my overwhelm take over and it caused me to be a less than fun roommate (to put it mildly).

I recently brought up this moment with one of my former roommates and apologised for my behaviour, as I had carried around all this shame for how I responded to what should have been a fun roommate bonding experience.

Funnily enough, she did not even remember us getting a tree that year, so I guess my obnoxiousness over what I thought was a big deal was not as horrible as I thought. But oh, the shame I carried around for years when I would think about that experience before my ADHD diagnosis.

I wish I had the language of ADHD during that moment so I could have thoughtfully communicated my concerns and asked for support in a way that could have enabled us all to enjoy the beautiful Christmas tree in our house.

I now realise that the tree incident also happened the same winter that I struggled to get my work done in a timely manner, as our work involved a lot of reading over what felt like a long time (overwhelm and boredom kicked in).

I went into hyperfocus at the end of that time period and got everything done in what my colleagues viewed as an unfathomable timeframe. And, let's be honest, it was the late 1990s and Making the Band was much more engaging than my actual work (and we didn't have on demand TV so if I missed the episode, I missed it!).

The reality is that I love having ADHD and being what my kids like to call ADHDtastic™. I wouldn't change my different wired brain in any way, and this journey has led me to do the work I now realise I was always meant to do (even though this career path didn't exist when I was younger).

I love being an ADHD Coach and entrepreneur, and I love the freedom and novelty that this career offers me. My clients keep me on my toes and I feel so honoured to be part of their ADHD journeys, and I am continually learning about ADHD so my love of learning muscle gets a workout every day.

Do I wish I was diagnosed earlier? Yes and no. Yes, as an earlier diagnosis would have saved me from so many struggles and challenges, but also no, as my many years as an undiagnosed ADHDer provides me with perspective, empathy and understanding for my clients, many of whom are late diagnosed as well.

I do believe that the earlier we can diagnose someone with ADHD, the faster they can begin to craft lives that align with their ADHD rather than working against it.

Living with ADHD is a journey, but it can also be one hell of a ride if you are willing to embrace it so you too can become ADHDtastic™.

"The only person you are destined to become is the person you decide to be."

-Ralph Waldo Emerson-

CHAPTER 17

Laughing Through The Chaos: My ADHD Journey

By Robert Powell

Hi, I am Rob,

This book is about the funny aspects of ADHD. They (not sure who) say life is a tragic comedy. I think humour is a very natural human reaction to the absurdity of certain situations. As the saying goes, you would cry if you didn't laugh!

I struggled to think of a funny story when asked to write this chapter, but to be honest, that's not because there aren't any, just that they seem like such normal occurrences that they become normal. Secondly, some of the stories are funny, but certainly not at the time! That's one of the downsides to having this thing; we often berate ourselves for our "failings," but we really should not. We didn't get to choose the source code when downloading our internal software!

So, some of the symptoms of ADHD are inattention to details, poor working memory, hyper-focusing on the wrong stuff, and so on. See if you can identify some of the symptoms in this story:

The Hilarious Brick Tinting Blunder That Led to Success"

So, I run my own business. I provide a service to repair damage to new surfaces.

Think French polishing but for a wide range of surfaces.

One service I provide is called brick tinting. Sometimes people get extensions, and the new brickwork doesn't match. I can apply a tint to the bricks to permanently change their colour so that the bricks match the old ones.

I received an inquiry from a frustrated builder. His client wasn't happy as the new extension bricks did not match! I did a site visit, but I was very busy at the time, and I didn't really want the job at that time, to be honest. Also, there were some technical challenges regarding the type of brick. I made my excuses and told him I could not do the job.

He persisted over the course of the next three months pestering me to try and do a sample to see if it was possible to tint the bricks. I finally gave in and said I'd go and give the sample a go. A sample is where I mix the colours up without the permanent stain and do one or two square meters. He wasn't going to be onsite, and we agreed that I just go whenever I had the time.

So one day I had some free time and attended the house. I drove to the road, saw the house with the wrong colour bricks, and began the sample. I'm a bit of a perfectionist, so I truly hyper-focused on the task at hand and got a really good sample. Proud of myself, I took some photos and proceeded home.

When I got home, I messaged the builder with the photos. I was quite proud of the accurate brick samples. I was a little concerned when I saw the message had been read, but there was no reply. I immediately began to think he thought it was crap or he wasn't happy with the match. Ten minutes went by before his reply came back, and it wasn't the one I was expecting or hoping for.

"That's not my house."

I'd only performed a brick tinting sample on the wrong house! The wrong house, on the same street, that had very similar brick issues!

My heart sank, and I felt like an absolute muppet! What's worse about the situation was that when I was working on this wrong house, I could see the correct property three doors up and was thinking, "Huh, so crazy that there is another property with the same brick colours on this street, there might be another job on this street later!" - I just didn't register it at all! Firstly, I suffer from a shocking memory because of ADHD, and secondly, I was so hyper-focused on doing a great job that I just didn't explore the possibility of it being the wrong house!

But you know what? The more times I told this story, the more people laughed, and I realised no harm came from it, and it was pretty funny! I ended up getting the job and solving the issues I procrastinated over, and it ended up being a success several months later!

Mother's Day ADHD Mishap

All right, brace yourself for a classic ADHD adventure!

Picture this: I was a teenager, and my brother and I were on a family trip when, lo and behold, we both forgot about Mother's Day. Oops, typical ADHD move!

We were in a panic mode, scrambling to find a last-minute gift in a village with limited shopping options. As we wandered around, we stumbled upon a card shop—a beacon of hope!

I hatched a plan. I told my brother to distract our mum while I raced into the store to find the perfect card.

Time was ticking, so I rushed to the mother section, scanning for a suitable one.

Finally, I spotted something fitting and snatched it up in a heartbeat. We quickly signed the card, thinking we were pulling off a last-minute miracle.

The next day, we presented our masterpiece to our mum with the obligatory chocolates. Expecting appreciation, we got hit with a sarcastic bombshell!

She exclaimed, "Oh, that's soooo nice of you!"

The tone in her voice revealed that something was amiss. With an amused grin, she revealed the card's front to us.

And there it was, our ADHD special: "You are like a mother to me."

We couldn't help but burst into laughter. We inadvertently gave her a card that made her feel like a super-mum extraordinaire! Thankfully, she took it all in good humour and teased us about it forever.

Lesson learned: Read the front of the card before you get carried away with ADHD-induced haste!

From that day on, our family had an epic Mother's Day story filled with laughs, love, and a touch of ADHD charm. After all, life is more fun when you embrace the quirks and share the laughter!

"Digging Deep: My Eccentric Dad, ADHD, and the Hilarious Burial Mishap"

My dad was a bit of a character and, dare I say it, a bit eccentric.

Sadly, he died before I got a diagnosis of ADHD because I am 100 per cent sure he had ADHD.

I could have probably written a book on him alone! We became mates in my early adulthood, as we were very alike. I think we both understood each other's struggles intuitively.

I worked in his business in my early twenties for a year or so. He had a plant refurbishing business, spray painting diggers, excavators, etc. He had a yard with some units at the time. At the time, he was living at the yard in a static caravan.

I was used to my dad asking me to do all sorts of unusual things, like the time he asked me to Dremel his tooth, but maybe that's another story!

I arrived early one morning before the other lads came in.

When I saw my dad, he said, "I need you to do something for me, but you can't ask what it is."

I mean, how do you respond to something like that?

"I want you to go to that land behind the building and dig me a hole ye big by ye big." He postured with his hands to display the "exact" dimensions.

Now, before you go down that road, this hole wasn't human-sized, so this wasn't a mafia-related episode, but still, at this point, I had no idea what the purpose of this task was! But also, it was pointless to ask!

Rather begrudgingly, in a sort of "Kevin the teenager" manner, I sulked off to dig this hole, "ye big by ye big."

Satisfied I had performed this duty, I returned to my dad, whence he served me with his second nonsensical request.

"I want you to go to the boot of my car and take the bag, but don't look in it. Take it to the hole and bury it, but make sure you make it look nice."

I mean, my imagination is running wild now. Is my dad some kind of drugs lord? Is this a huge stash of cash, etc., etc.?

I'm not sure at what point this occurred, but I dropped the bag, and it tore. Contrary to my imagination, no money fell out or bizarre white powder; I could only see a bit of fur poking out. As I investigated further, the suspicious item appeared to be a dead cat. As I looked at my dad, he said, "Don't ask! Just go bury it."

So, I went to the sacred burial ground behind the building and proceeded with the task. I said a little (comedy) prayer in my mind and had a chuckle. The hole looked suitably sized, so I placed the poor cat in the hole, filled it in, and carefully placed the turf back. I walked back to my dad, who proceeded to tell me that he had met a woman, and her cat had recently died, and as an act of good faith, he had promised to find a nice spot to bury him and that he would take some photos. He went to the site and began to take some photos.

He returned somewhat animated and verbally expressed some swear words.

"You can't leave it like that!"

"I thought I had done a good job!"

"Come and have a look!"

As dusk slowly became morning, with the dew glistening on the grass, you could just see the few inches of the black furry tail protruding from the grave!

Now, I'm not sure whose ADHD was responsible for this. Was it me for not following the instructions "ye big, by ye big", or was it my dad's for failing to "plan" this project, or mine for "failing to complete the project? Nevertheless, it was pretty funny!

When my dad passed, I found some photos, and I had no idea what they were at the time, but it turned out they were the first takes of this hilarious moment where the cat's tail was sticking out of the ground. It made me laugh, for sure. Maybe it was his way of still having a chuckle at this moment!

I miss my dad, and one of my regrets was that I was not able to share my diagnosis with him. It could have quite literally been the missing puzzle for him. He spent his life chronically disorganised and beating himself up for not living up to whatever he thought he should be. Getting a diagnosis would have given him, at the very least, some kind of self-acceptance.

I named my business after him. His name was David Barry Powell, and his business was DB Powell Coachbuilders. My business is DB Powell Repairs, and I repair a heap of things that are typically too difficult to replace.

"Believe in yourself and all that you are. Know that there is something inside you that is greater than any obstacle."

-Christian D. Larson-

CHAPTER 18

ADHD And My Journey To Self-Acceptance

By Emma Sails

The two most impactful days of my life so far have been the day I had my son and the day I found out what ADHD is. Sometimes it's debatable which of those things has had the most impact on my life.

I was 35 years old and speaking with a money coach who was helping me overcome my life-long toxic relationship with money (which was, of course, linked to my toxic relationship with food, work, and so on…). She asked me if I'd ever considered that I might have ADHD, and I laughed. In my mind at that point, ADHD was something that "naughty boys in school" have… how could I, a successful businesswoman, have ADHD?? Well, she sent me a list of 25 ADHD traits, and I could strongly identify with 22 of them. A few of them brought me to tears, and for the first time ever, I realised that there could be an explanation for almost all the things I hated (strong word, but true) about myself.

The more I read about ADHD, the more I resonated with it. The more I realised that the teenage version of me, who was diagnosed at 15 with neurosis and spent most of her secondary school years hiding had a genuine reason.

There WAS something different in my mind from the minds of my peers and it WASN'T nothing.

I wasn't just being silly, trying to attract attention or making excuses… this was a REAL THING.

To me, that was enormous to find out. After years of believing I was 'just rubbish', the relief was astounding, and ADHD became my passion. I was joyful in telling my friends that the affectionately named "Emma-time" I run on is caused by time blindness. I was confident in telling clients that I often didn't get back to them until just before a deadline because I find it easier to focus in a crisis. I had an exceptionally emotional conversation with my Mum about how suddenly my whole life made sense. It sounds dramatic and did really feel that way… but it was still such an enormous relief.

There was no doubt in my mind that this was my answer. 2.5 years later, I am waiting for a diagnosis for combined ADHD and ASD through the NHS, and I am in a better place mentally than I was. I get so frustrated at the number of people who describe the diagnosis of ADHD and other neurodivergent conditions as giving yourself a label; to me, they are so much more than that. ADHD is validation that I am not rubbish, that there is a reason why I really struggle with some things and that there is a way to get help. Why wouldn't anyone want that for themselves or for their child?

Not long after I started learning about ADHD, I became an accredited coach, and I work with parents of neurodivergent children to help them overcome guilt and resentment, learn to acknowledge how awesome they are and learn how to communicate with their children. Raising a neurodivergent child is very challenging, and I know from my own experiences how much we put ourselves through mentally.

As parents, we are our children's safe places and their role models.

If we treat ourselves with kindness and respect and give ourselves the time and space to address our needs, our children will learn to do the same.

There are a lot of ways that ADHD helped me in my career before I even knew it existed. Before I trained as a coach, I ran a successful bookkeeping business for several years and before that worked at an accountancy practice where I was such a valued member of their bookkeeping department that it took me 3 attempts at handing in my notice to actually leave (people-pleasing tendencies and a lack of boundaries have a lot to answer for…).

My job at the accountants I worked at was a rollercoaster from start to finish; I started working there at 19 and finally left 13 years later. Life dealt me quite a few difficult hands in that time, and the resolve and defiance that ADHD has given me helped me to pull through and keep my job each time. Just before I was 'temporarily' transferred into the bookkeeping department, aged 21, I had been through a very rough breakup. I was given a warning at work, but I managed to turn things around in a short space of time and actually received a wage increase 3 months later (doubt me, and I will fight to prove you wrong…).

However, the manager of the bookkeeping department had only seen the struggles I'd had and there was no way she wanted me on her team; it seemed that turning up hungover and carrying bags of pasties, then spending the day browsing the internet isn't great for your image at work. She reluctantly agreed, and then 2 months later I'd figured out how to cut down a weekly task she was doing from a full day's work into 2 hours (yay for problem-solving skills and out-of-the-box thinking!) and she refused to let me go back into my old department.

I have always been very open with my bookkeeping clients about the way I work, even before I knew why. Clients knew that with me, the job would always be thorough and that the deadline would always be met. One of my clients, who I still do some work for, always brings her accounting records in the month after her year-end. Every year until this year, nine months later I sat down to do the work just before the deadline. This year I emailed the accounts to her two months after she gave me the records, and she rang me to check everything was ok!

In my personal life, ADHD has given me a lot to laugh about over the years. I have always been good at laughing at myself, but since I learned about ADHD my laughter is so much less critical than it was, and I don't berate myself anywhere near as much.

The ability to laugh at myself is so important, but it has taken quite a lot of work to accept that. Yes, sometimes I don't think things through as they're happening, but it's just another amusing story and another part of the awesome person that I am. Someone rarely gets hurt, and it is often something very insignificant, so the days of making myself miserable for getting distracted and forgetting things are long gone. I thrive on making people laugh and so now instead of endless apologies I tend to make a joke of it when I turn up late to meetings because I've accidentally left the car at Tesco or lost my laptop.

I know it's OK to forget things and that it's normal for my brain, so I can accept it much more easily. I find that if you can start a meeting with laughter and positivity it always makes for a better meeting, no matter what the subject is.

One of my favourite ADHD stories to tell is how a few years ago when I was moving house, I decided to clear out the attic and get rid of a load of stuff I'd been holding onto. It was a big step for me because I don't like letting go of things and still had all of my old school diaries, posters from my teenage bedroom and all sorts. I hyper focused on the task, of course, and cleared out loads in around 5 hours. I'd casually been throwing bin bags and empty boxes down the hatch from the loft all afternoon when I realised I desperately needed to eat and go to the bathroom. On turning around, I noticed that I'd completely filled the loft hatch with boxes and bags, piled down the stepladder to the floor, and inadvertently trapped myself in the loft. It took a while to dig myself out, but you'll be glad to know that I did make it to the bathroom on time.

I've also come to appreciate, rather than be offended by, the looks of amazement and confusion from friends and family when I explain why I've approached something in a different way than what was expected.

For example, it is perfectly logical to lean a petrol strimmer up against a wall for storage because then the fuel cap is upright, so it won't leak. Yes, there is a stand on the back of it for lying it down and storing it horizontally... but that might not have been a stand. It might have just been some metal attached to the back of the strimmer for another purpose. How was I to know...?

Learning about ADHD and neurodiversity has truly been a revelation for me and has been fundamental in my journey of self-acceptance. Spreading awareness and helping other adults and future generations accept neurodiversity and adjust to it is where my future lies.

I hope that my story can help to give people the confidence to explore their own neurodiversity and learn that no matter how their brain works it's OK. There is a massive amount of support out there, and an awesome community of like-minded people who will make you feel accepted and help you believe that you're awesome just as you are. (1576 Words)

CHAPTER 19

Party Girl ADHD Success

By Kim Sheppard

Hi, I'm Kim, the fabulous 63-year-old party girl! Yeah, you heard that right! Passionate about animals, have several rescue cats and am a big believer in giving back in life. I have always been a YES person and supported whoever and whenever I could. I am grounded, grateful and blessed that I have succeeded in life without no qualifications from school to my name. Who needs 'em? But hey, I've succeeded in life anyway!

I am highly energetic and have partied every weekend of my long life! And recently, I decided to add life coach, counsellor, hypnotherapist, and NLP enthusiast to my resume. So, naturally, I needed an ADHD diagnosis, which the NHS was happy to offer... in a few years. Well, no time to wait around, darling! I went private and, surprise surprise, already knew I had ADHD. It's like knowing your own superpower, right? Turns out, it's combination type ADHD—double the fun!

Let me tell you about my rollercoaster career journey!

I have worked in law to IT, and out of nowhere, I opened a flowers shop without a single day's training, Crimson Rose in SE18 and sold it 18 years later, that was a huge challenge as I went from earning £7k a month to opening a "start-up" company, I turned that around and sold it when I made six figures.

Oh, and I'm not just a one-trick pony. I am also the owner and co-founder of **www.floralfrog.co.uk** and also Retail Frog. I am also the owner of kim-e-fleurs.co.uk where I still undertake floral work and wedding work. I have also started my Coaching business recognising-change.co.uk. I also have a small portfolio of properties. Bought a repossession in Spain with no windows, doors, running water, electrics but they didn't stop me from renovating it with my partner and selling it on for a profit. Who needs sleep, am I right?

I WAS TOLD at SCHOOL I would be a good "CHECKOUT GIRL", no I would not!!, since which time I have

Danced with the Masai Mara, watched the sunset in Sydney, fed orangutans in Borneo, watched the waterfalls in Niagara, And that's just the beginning! I partied hard in New York, soaked up the sun in Barbados, and celebrated my 40th birthday in Vegas, baby! Whales in Hawaii, an island in Panama, partied in New York, spent 4 months in India travelling, been to the slums of Bombay, and travelled at least 50 per cent of Europe. Had a boat ride through the waters of Costa Rica, partied hard in Miami, bought emeralds in Columbia, slept in a shed in Tasmania and so many more exciting travel experiences. I loved every moment. It has helped me to see the world and the diversity that we have around us. I have never judged anyone and am happy to accept everyone's opinion on how they see life. I take on board everyone's individuals' beliefs and never put my own on them.

So how did I know that I have ADHD? I didn't. How did I succeed at most things I did? Not sure, it certainly wasn't because I studied because I would never focus on much and school certainly didn't interest me. I started work at 13 and since that time I navigated my way through life.

I was always looking for the next best well-paid job. At the age of 19, I decided I would become a legal secretary because at that time the pay was £10 per hour and I really needed that £10 because I need to buy clothes every week, that's definitely an obsession, my love for fashion. All my money was spent back then, we got paid weekly, and Top Shop at Oxford Circus was my go-to place.

I had NO experience of being a legal secretary, but that never stopped me, I would say "YES" to almost everything and hope for the best. I got asked to leave as I was "NO GOOD" at the job, but I never gave up. I carried on until I was excellent at the job and went on to work for some of the biggest names in Law including Princess Di's solicitors. I worked for a Hungarian Lawyer, a very old man who insisted I was a "shorthand secretary". I had no clue about shorthand but never told him.

I worked in a typing pool, so each time I was asked to take a letter, I had to scribble the words down as quickly as possible and ask the girls not to talk to me until I had recited the letter, as I had to remember it (I done pretty good at that), but I was very young then. Since that time and where I am now, my memory has got much worse! Losing things, OMG, I can literally make a cuppa, lose it, and make another one, without realising I had already made one. Keys, they are another story!!!! I'm sure many of you can relate to those!

My other experience was with my florist friend who said to me one day "If I die before you, will you turn up at my funeral?" I said to her, "Why are you saying that"? she said to me, "Well it's your ADHD; you will probably forget"!!!! that's been a joke with us ever since I was diagnosed....

I've always been a sensitive soul and had some very sad times in life, most of those times are to do with animal cruelty. My heart and soul really do belong to animals.

I remember one time I was working in my flower shop. Each day, I would pet and feed a dog called "Baron". He was a pitbull, a beautiful beige sweetheart. His owner was a heroin addict. 3 days before he died, the man came to me and said, "If I die will you take my dog"? of course, I would but had no clue he was literally going to die so soon.

The dog ended up in the hands of another drug dealer, and I was beside myself. I put out a REWARD for the dog and during the next week, I was handed a dog in between making funeral flowers and asked to hand over the money! There was a beautiful ending to this story as I re-homed him to a wonderful man, and they had a wonderful friendship until Baron recently passed away.

I also broke into a flat in my local area as I was told a man was punching a kitten in the face. So, my friend and I broke in, called him a name I can't mention here, I ran up the road with my NOW Polly pockets in my arms, drove my van home and she is still with me today.

I was arrested in my old flower shop because I didn't pay the rent one month after 11 years of never missing a payment, the roof was leaking, and the owner told me to "F OFF", he closed my shop with a lot of funeral flowers in so I was beside myself. I have NEVER been aggressive, but he called the police and told them I was abusing him, I was arrested, and held up against the wall for all the locals to see. Taken to the local police station and put in a cell.

I told the policeman I was "claustrophobic", and he said they all said that.

I was crying and I'm sure all the criminals had a bloody good laugh! I was, of course, let go. I have never been violent or otherwise. It was the nasty landlord. However, they turned out to my benefit as I got a shop over the road in a much better location!

So, how did I even think I had ADHD? I have lived my life at 100 miles per hour, I have literally done most things I set out to do. I never knew where my confidence came from. I had no examinations to my name, no family support or handouts, I just knew that I had to succeed, and I would succeed. I have always been proactive, hard-working and have a never give up attitude. I knew what I wanted in my life, and I knew that I had to work hard to get it. I have had so many jobs without no experience, and it really is a testament that a "piece of paper with your name and an accreditation stamp" doesn't mean any more than HANDS-ON EXPERIENCE, CONFIDENCE and BELIEF IN SELF. I believe we all have the power within to achieve much in life, you just have to believe it and when you do you can "live it". I am a big believer in the fact that if you can resonate with someone who has similar conditions to yourself, you can support them and that is what I am currently doing. I love to talk to other neurodivergent people, I feel at home with them.

I have a different song in my head each time I lay my head on the pillow, that is my thinking time, I have the traffic coming from everywhere, it can be debilitating but I have learnt to live with it.

Thank you, ADHD for being the driving force behind my success

I thank you ADHD, for being by my side throughout my life, for excelling me forward and reaching heights I never would have imagined.

You have given me the energy to thrive and live my life to the fullest. I don't believe I could have achieved so much without you!

I also thank you, ADHD, for giving me unbelievable energy to continue my quest for living my life in the "party mood". People really do not believe my age and the energy that I possess.

I am all about helping other neurodivergence to see the positive in their uniqueness and not to let others pass on their perceptions, we are all unique, and I am proud of everything that I have achieved. I never thought I would say that about myself, BUT I have learnt to really appreciate ME and my ADHD. And believe me, and there's more to come! Embrace your quirks, peeps—own your awesomeness!

CHAPTER 20

Relatable & Laughable: A Rollercoaster Of An ADHD Experience

By Beth Thomas

When the opportunity to co-author a chapter within this fantastic project first presented itself, I felt so many things. Excitement and honour at the thought of writing about something that ignites passion for me, then total paralysing fear.

Naturally, I proceeded to arrive promptly at procrastination station long enough for the unhelpful rumination to become louder than anything else in my busy brain (for any of your wondering, yes of course this procrastination took me right up to the 11th hour before the deadline…).

So much to say, yet no idea how to form it into something cohesive.

Who am I to have the audacity to take up space here?

Are my words even that valuable?

What if everyone hates it and my courageous attempt at vulnerability is ridiculed?

How do I even begin to share a snippet of my life in such a way that readers will laugh, connect with and gain benefit from my words?

Then I caught myself, I noticed all those old fears and limiting beliefs holding me hostage. Preventing me from even attempting to contribute something that could have been helpful to others who may be struggling.

Then I remembered that I'm not doing this to be liked, or to seek approval. I'm writing for the recovering perfectionists, the lost, confused & frustrated. I'm writing for those still feeling stuck or resentful that their beautiful brain thinks differently to the other 80% of the world. This is to show you all that ADHD isn't shameful, it can be shiny, special, and sometimes side-splittingly hilarious.

And so we begin.

I was never diagnosed as a child. I never quite fit in anywhere either. Looking back with the knowledge I have now, ADHD stares so plainly back from my history. School reports peppered with comments regarding my focus (or lack thereof) and talkative nature. Many new friends made but few sustained throughout the years. Perpetual issues with time management, forgetfulness, being 'too loud' and 'too abrasive'. Quite frankly it seemed I was only ever 'too much' or 'not enough' of anything at any one time.

Despite this, I ended up being labelled as 'gifted and talented' from primary school, which if you aren't familiar with this term, essentially just meant higher academic expectations from adults with less support to achieve. What did this create? To those of you who guessed savage performance anxiety, you would be correct! By the time I hit secondary school there was a permanent lingering shadow of anxiety around my performance with very little awareness of what I could do to ease it. So instead, I learnt to mask and compensate.

It wasn't all pure misery though, just like the classic British summer weather - there were patches of sunlight shining through the grey, dreary and dreadful.

Thinking of hilarious and cringey stories for this chapter wasn't the problem- those were plenty.

As a child, my family used to despair at both the speed and volume I could talk. I loved & still love talking. Often, it would be about the things that interested me the most, however I could still talk about things that I didn't know much about and still 'talk the hind legs off a donkey' as they'd say. It wasn't that they didn't want to hear what I had to say, it was more an issue that they usually couldn't keep up with the pace of it to process everything in time.

Naturally I would take great offence at what seemed to be a lack of interest in the random ramblings of my brain, so we needed to figure out a solution. My mum was the genius thinker for this one- she created a 'pause' button which still works to this day!

Any time a family member needs a break to digest my external monologue, they hold up an imaginary remote control to me and say 'pause' and just like that, I will quite literally pause what I'm saying and doing for a short while until they hit 'play'.

This has baffled anyone who has seen it happen in action, although interestingly when I explain the purpose their usual response is 'oh that makes so much sense, I wish I'd have known you come with a pause button when we first met!'.

To encapsulate this little quip, I shall complete it with one of my favourite reviews I've ever received about myself.

This coming from a very special person who when they first met me, many moons ago, said, "I like having a conversation with Beth because she is quite happy to talk to herself so you don't have to invest much energy into the conversation as she'll keep it going for both of you". (Don't worry, I've since learnt to develop my conversational skills so I'm talking *with* people and not just *at* them!).

Interception hasn't always been a strength of mine. For those unfamiliar, this is the ability to know what's going on internally i.e. are we cold, thirsty, hungry etc? For me it's often not realising I need to go to the bathroom until I'm on the verge of needing a mop, bucket & fresh underwear. This was often cringey at school, however more recently caught me off guard when I went to Poland with my partner.

We organised a day trip which involved a 2-hour minibus journey to site, which for many people sounds like a walk in the park. For me however, it was anything but. About 40 minutes away from our destination, I started to need the bathroom. I felt too awkward and rude to ask if we could pull over so I gritted my teeth and wished for the best (not the wisest decision as it turns out). By the time we arrived I was literally sweating from the energy it had taken to keep myself composed and desperately shuffled past every other passenger to launch myself off the bus and into the direction of the WC sign I had seen at the start of the car park. In this time, I forgot to remember my phone or purse (which my partner kept safe thankfully) and didn't hear the guide shouting from the bus.

Turns out, he was shouting the directions to the correct bathroom as this one was not part of the museum we were attending.

Consequently, I had to play a game of desperate charades with the lovely bathroom attendant who didn't speak English to try and explain that I didn't have any money to pay but I was desperate. I exchanged my rings (which were borrowed from my sister!) in the hope this would cover the fees I couldn't produce with coins. She must have pitied my desperate, sweaty face as she kindly allowed me entry. By this time, I was late for the museum, had no phone to contact my partner for directions and didn't know where I was supposed to be. I wandered around the huge car park for a few minutes to figure out the right way to go. I reached the right place finally, but it took me a few more minutes to find familiar faces from the same bus we had taken. At this point it was too late to rescue my sisters' rings and pay the kind lady, so I had to wait half the day until a short break where I could dash back and pay her the money- hoping she would still have the rings. Thankfully she did and I didn't have to awkwardly explain to my sister that she needed new jewellery. The ride back home, as I am sure you can all imagine, proceeded to be rather cringey with the other passengers finding it absolutely hilarious that I had nearly floored some of them WWE style in order to make it to a bathroom.

Moving swiftly on as we don't have the word count for our well known and beloved tangents. I'd like to share some stories about my working memory (or lack thereof should we say!).

I forget many things, except anything completely random and probably unhelpful unless I were to enter a pub quiz every night of the week. I frequently forgot deadlines at school, forgot to set alarms for work and so ended up late at least once to every job I've ever had, I (still) forget I have very good friends who have pesky recurring things like birthdays on set days of the year.

My most recent faux pas in this department was forgetting to pick my dear mum up from work a few months back despite me setting an alarm, having a conversation on the phone with her that very day about picking her up and thinking on two separate occasions 'I must not forget to pick my mum up today'. For some reason, I finished my final appointment of the day and my brain decided we were done! When the alarm went off, I sat bemused for a moment and thought, 'oh well, if this alarm was for something important, I'm sure I'll remember at some point'. I did not remember. It wasn't until my sister called me about something that it jigged my memory and I realised I was supposed to be in the car! Luckily, my wonderful mum knows me well and we were able to laugh about this.

Historically, my poor memory would frequently give my friends metaphoric grey hair at university. I forgot almost every deadline in my first two years of the degree (there were only three years of this degree in total). The worst one was first year; I distinctly remember calling up my best friend in a state of sheer panic and emotional dysregulation as I had suddenly remembered a short reading summary I had not written for a deadline the next morning at midday. As she was essentially my executive functioning for the duration of my degree, she begrudgingly walked me to the library where we proceeded to pull an all-nighter (fuelled by desperation, sugar and probably too much caffeine) in order to get this assignment researched, written, referenced, proof-read and submitted all within 12 hours.

I haven't always made the best decisions when it comes to friends and role models to spend my time around. When you're a people pleasing lost soul looking for a place to belong- you can find yourself in less than healthy environments.

However I am incredibly grateful that I have a few special people who have stuck by me throughout the years of risky, impulsive, cringey and downright ridiculous situations.

I did also mention at the start of this chapter that I would show you ADHD doesn't have to be shameful and I hope these small snapshots of hilarity give you an insight into how face-palm moments like these can be chucklesome to reflect back on.

Of course- it hasn't always been easy to look back and laugh at moments like these. There was a time when this would be painfully embarrassing to reflect and I couldn't do so without entering the spiral of ruminating shame. If you're still there and you're reading this- it doesn't have to always be this way. I can't tell you what will work specifically for you, but I can tell you that if you figure that out, you'll be able to embrace every element of your wonderful uniqueness and harness those individual strengths to become the core of everything you do.

Once I learnt how to forgive myself, be kind and compassionate to myself, learn how to lean into support for my lesser strengths and structure my world around my strongest strengths, I stopped flying into the sun and burning myself out and instead found a way to thrive, soaring high into the skies with confidence and clarity.

Now, I get to do what I LOVE. I talk for a living! Well, actually I'm a coach first so I mostly ask curious questions, though part of my work is helping to educate others so they understand how they too can thrive **with** their brains instead of against them.

I will complete this brief chapter with a note to anyone who resonates with anything I've mentioned.

You are important, seen, heard, valued and special. You matter. Your thoughts matter. Your feelings matter. You have a uniqueness that 80% of the world will never have just by your very design. If you make yourself smaller for others to 'fit in', the world misses out on the unique, marvellous beauty that is you. (word count: 2086)

CHAPTER 21

The ADHD Realisation

By Emma Whalley

Diagnosed later in life, I first realised that, yes! I think I have ADHD after listening to a coaching call on replay on the way home from my sister's house. The two-and-a-half-hour drive home let me listen to this coaching call and take in the revelation I was having without distraction!

I'm usually doing four different things at once. The coaching calls were usually listened to while I was cooking, cleaning, and generally flitting between rooms in my house, forgetting what I was meant to be doing. However, I can only concentrate on listening by engaging in another activity simultaneously. Mundane things like cleaning are good activities to help me concentrate on audio.

I'd just been for a weekend at my sister's, where she had been telling me (again!) that she thinks I'm autistic. I didn't think it was autism, but finally admitted that something was different about me. She'd been banging on about this for years, so I thought I'd start to listen during a lovely 6-course taster menu meal. Probably the only time she's had me in one place for that amount of time! (We were one of the first in the restaurant and the last ones out!)

This is why it was such a lightning bolt to my brain when I listened to four other female entrepreneurs talk about their ADHD.

The things they do, how they flit from one thing to the next, how their brain works with ideas and takes action. The hyperfocus, then the burnout. 'Oh my goodness, it's exactly me', I thought. When I got home, I texted my sister, "I have ADHD!"

I'd admitted there was something different about me to my sister while I was at hers for the weekend, but I'd known that since primary school. I liked it! There's nothing wrong with being different. I still like it. I used to think and there's nothing wrong with me. It's other people!

I looked at other people and thought it would be boring to have what I thought was a much slower brain than mine. They just seemed to be able to think about one thing at a time, do one thing at a time and take ages to think of an idea and make the decision to go ahead and do it.

I'd been told for decades by high school friends, university mates, friends and work colleagues that they loved the way I think. I can think out of the box. I can look at situations and see an overview as if from a Bird's Eye view. I could come up with ideas for businesses in a flash! It's like I don't even have to think. It just comes out of my mouth.

But the more I looked into ADHD, the more I realised about myself. I've now found out so much through research and talking to other ADHDers. Especially women with ADHD, as it is displayed differently in women. I had been previously diagnosed with chronic depressive disorder, and now I've been told that was a misdiagnosis, just classic ADHD.

Going through life with ADHD, you do some funny stuff! When I look back, I think, that's so ADHD! Here are some funny ADHD stories that have happened in my time.

Being Forgetful:

I got assessed for ADHD through a clinical psychiatrist on the NHS. The assessment is thorough with lots of questions, including, Do you find you are forgetful? and Do you lose things often?

For these, I told him I often forgot things like where my keys were and find them randomly in the fridge! I often forget where I've put my drink as I'll have been flitting around the house and forget I made one. Sometimes my husband finds my cup of tea in the microwave the day after I've attempted to warm it up - Forgot where it was, then forget that I put it in the microwave to warm up! The other evening, he came into the lounge with a cold bowl of dried-up porridge say, 'What's this?'. I thought I'd had breakfast that morning, but I must have forgotten! Out of sight, out of mind! Even if it's for 2 minutes in the microwave. This is typical me, typical ADHD.

Anyway, back to the ADHD assessment. One of the things they ask after they have been diagnosed and before prescribing medication is about your blood pressure and heart rate. I'd got myself prepared for the appointment well, I thought. I'd been to the pharmacy, and they'd done the tests for me. They'd written them down, and I'd put the bit of paper in my phone.

So when the psychiatrist asked for my results, I said, "Oh, I'll need to find my phone. I've lost it somewhere". I then run out of the room, running around the house screaming for my husband to help me find my phone. I'm frantic!

Then I remember! I was on my phone on a video call speaking to the psychiatrist! After a face-palm action, I slump my way upstairs and admit to him, "Oops, I'm on the phone with you! It's here!"

He said, "Yep, classic ADHD!" I would have been mortified, but the relief of someone understanding and spotting it as a normal ADHD trait was at least a bit reassuring!

Lack of Focus:

I run my own business helping women in business get themselves online, training them in social media marketing and online business strategies. I love my work, but sometimes I can find myself procrastinating when there is a boring task I need to do.

And my boring tasks are emails! I have a fear of emails because, for one, it's very hard to read them, and two, I can't understand them and three, my God, if they include forms, it's impossibly boring and hard to do.

I can't even remember when the boring email was this time that I was wanting to avoid! But I ended up creating a whole course and planner that took hours to do over a long weekend just to avoid the forms I had to do.

The email was a 5-10 min job, but I just couldn't muster any enthusiasm for it, so it didn't get done. Until 1 hour before the deadline for it! What can I say? There's no dopamine hit in form filling is there?

Bluntly Honest:

Another time, I was with my sister. Sorry, many of these stories are with my sister!

I think she's the only person close enough to me to point things out and can laugh about them. Other people must just sit there bewildered about what's just gone on when I do stuff like this to them!

We were in Hamburg around Christmas time. We'd been to the Christmas markets and been on bus and boat tours around the city. Lovely times with my Dad and my sister.

One evening, before getting ready for dinner at a traditional German restaurant, Rosie and I were having a drink at the bar and chatting. Rosie is the person that had been on at me to look at some sort of neurodivergent condition I had. So over drinks, she was pointing out that I need not to be so blunt as people can take it the wrong way. I just see it as honesty, but I say I understand, and we go upstairs to get ready to go out.

Rosie had put on a new dress that we'd bought another time when out shopping in Birmingham. She came into the bathroom while I was putting my makeup on and said "Ta-da, do you like it!?" I loved the dress, it was stunning on her, and she has such a lovely figure. But she had no make-up on or not much at all. I said, 'I like everything but the face.' Meaning, are you putting some makeup on? It wasn't the sort of dress where you'd only have slight makeup on. Well, she took offense but laughed because we'd literally just been talking about my blunt honesty and how it can come across as hurtful!

Oh, dear! I honestly don't mean it in a bad way. So, I offered to do her makeup, and she looked more stunning than the dress! I think she got over it eventually because now she asks me to do her make-up on occasion.

Impulsivity:

Oh my goodness, there's lots in this category! Like the time I decided to create a Facebook group for ADHD Women Entrepreneurs Support just five days after I was diagnosed myself!

The many times I've decided on nights out, I need to go home and just found myself leaving without anyone knowing.

The times I just book a trip the morning of the trip so I can escape life for 24 hours.

Times I've quit jobs when I've been so bored! I just can't work somewhere that doesn't give me excitement, lets me think outside the box and doesn't give recognition. Sounds like most places I worked in during my employed years! Thank goodness I'm now running my own business.

When I got the questionnaires from Adult ADHD Services before my assessment, one of the questions was, how many jobs have you had?

I pondered on this question, trying to count them all up. I reflected back to age 14 when I got my first job, then after uni, counting my jobs. Gosh, there was a lot! I counted 22! That was a new job every 1.3 years on average!

Wow! But the longest job I've done in my business, I'm proud to say. I started my business over 5 years ago and have successfully replaced and surpassed the income of my previous Marketing Manager role in employment. Plus, I managed to earn enough to help my husband cut his hours by half so he could be less stressed and be home more to look after my son, who has moderate to severe autism.

Thriving with ADHD in business:

I have to say, running my own business has been the making of me, and I feel all the other 21 job roles that went before it has helped me with the skills I need for business.

But more than that, it's helping my ADHD brain thrive! I can think of new ideas all the time and just do them. I've crafted my business so my brain can get excited each month about something. I run a brilliant membership that helps women with online business and marketing.

So, I deliver new training each month and help them with any screen share how-to sessions they need.

I also help people with their social media. And as you may have noticed, social media changes all the time. So for me, learning new things each month and progressing with the online business and social media world is great.

My Learnings and Advice:

I'd love to give some advice here, based on my experience. I've found that surrounding yourself with people like yourself is really helpful. I have networked for many years and like attracts like. When there's someone like you, make an effort to connect more with them.

You will gather a tribe of like-minded people. Whether you are a leader or not, being around people who get it is comforting. It was astounding that when I let people know I have ADHD, how many others have it too that I didn't know about?

Doing something I feel excited about keeps my dopamine levels firing better. I may still be forgetful, impulsive and lack focus (on boring stuff!), but I can accept myself for that.

Without ADHD, I don't think I would be as excitable. Without ADHD, I know I wouldn't be given all these amazing ideas. And I love it!

Another point I want to include is about medication. I am now on medication for ADHD, and it works brilliantly for me. Medication is actually one of the reasons why I sort a diagnosis. I put off being referred for ADHD for 18 months once I knew I had it (self-diagnosed). That changed when I was at one of the ADHD support group that Bernadette Ashton - ADHD Lancashire runs.

It was at the online meeting that the guest speaker said, it's not all about me. It's about Mr Whalley too! I live with my husband and son, and my ADHD affects them too. This was a new thought for me, allowing me to see how having more focus on the medication could help our lives.

My question back was about my ideas, though. I was worried that all these amazing ideas would disappear when I was on medication. And the answer was, 'No, you will still have all your ideas". The medication will just help you focus.

I was so pleased to hear that! And I can confirm I'm still like lightning with ideas and outside-the-box thinking. I still learn fast on interesting topics for me and have innovation. The medication is just brilliant for helping me stay on task and complete the ideas I start to take action on! Yippee!

Short Stories

Contributors to the book

I want to extend my heartfelt gratitude to each and every one of you for coming forward and bravely sharing your short stories about living with adult ADHD. Your willingness to open up and offer glimpses into your lives is not only commendable but also incredibly valuable.

Living with adult ADHD can be a daily struggle, and it often feels like an invisible battle. However, by sharing our stories, we shed light on the challenges, triumphs, and unique experiences that come with this condition. In doing so, we not only raise awareness but also create a sense of community and understanding.

Your stories serve as beacons of inspiration, offering hope to those who may be navigating the complexities of ADHD in adulthood for the first time. They remind us that we are not alone in our journeys, and there is strength in unity.

So, thank you for your courage, vulnerability, and the gift of your stories. Together, we can break down stigmas, foster empathy, and continue supporting one another on this remarkable journey of living with adult ADHD.

With gratitude and solidarity,

Bernadette

> *"In the middle of every difficulty lies opportunity."*
>
> -Albert Einstein-

New Start

By Rebecca Batstone

New job / New home / New Country!

In 1997 I was 25 years old, single, living in York and working as a store manager for Boots having qualified as a pharmacist two years earlier.

Even though it was early in my career I was already burnt out with the demand of running a store, managing staff and driving over an hour each way to and from work. Finding myself with a rare and unexpected week off work in October, I decided to head to Scotland to do some walking, reconnect with nature (my happy place) and decompress.

While there I decided on a whim that I was going to quit my job and move to Scotland, basically to wherever I could manage to find a new role first. When I got home the first job I saw advertised was in Stornoway in the Western Isles. I immediately phoned the number in the advert, spoke to the owner of the business who agreed to ring me back that evening. After a 2- hour conversation, mostly about music and not about running a pharmacy at all, he had persuaded me that the next time I got two days off together I should go and visit them and if they liked me and I liked them the job was mine. Needless to say, the rest is history!

On the 6th December 1997, after only ever visiting Stornoway once and before that only knowing where it was from the map on the weather forecast (!) I packed up my Citroen Saxo and with my cat drove 9 hours to Ullapool and boarded a ferry for Stornoway.

I spent 5 years living in the amazing Western Isles, met my best friend, had some fantastic experiences and laughs, connected with some wonderful crazy, kind, generous souls and when I left at the age of 30 had been privileged to experience living in one of the most beautiful, remote, exhilarating and picturesque special places in the world.

25 years later at the age of 50 - literally a whole lifetime again since I moved there, I was finally diagnosed ADHD. At last, my impulsivity and spontaneity had an explanation. Yes, ADHD can be frustrating and annoying and all of those other things but without it would I have had the courage to up sticks and move nearly 500 miles to somewhere I'd never visited before, almost certainly not. Do I regret it – not for one second! Some of my most enduring and positive memories and experiences came from living on Lewis and my best and more enduring friendships were forged there too.

Paul's Quirky Funeral Procession

By Paul Carter

I was a character known for my quirky sense of humour, even in the most challenging situations. In my mid-thirties, tragedy struck the family. Our beloved pet dog, Jess, had reached the end of her tail-wagging adventures and bid farewell to this world. The news of Jess's passing spread like wildfire, sending shockwaves of sorrow throughout the family.

I had always been a master of disguise, concealing my emotions behind a veil of humour. Grief had struck my heart, but I refused to let it consume me. With a mischievous gleam in my eye, I hatched a plan only I could devise.

Armed with Jess's lifeless body, I took it upon myself to organise a grand burial ceremony. However, this was not going to be an ordinary funeral. Oh no, I had something far more outrageous in mind.

I emerged from my front door carrying Jess's lifeless form. As I stepped onto the village road, I raised my voice to the heavens and shouted, "Bring out your dead! Bring out your dead!

The villagers, caught off guard by their zany neighbour parading through the streets, couldn't help but stop in their tracks. Some of them stared in confusion, while others burst into fits of laughter. The scene was nothing short of a circus itself.

I continued my grand procession, occasionally stopping to share a witty remark with the gathered onlookers.

The once sombre atmosphere of the village had transformed into a joyous spectacle, thanks to the absurdity of my mourning.

My family, who had initially questioned my sanity, watched from the front porch, their tears replaced with laughter. They realised that beneath my outlandish performance, I was trying to cope with the pain of losing Jess in my own unique way.

From that day forward, my peculiar send-off for Jess reminded my family and the village that grief doesn't have to be endured in silence. Sometimes, a little laughter can go a long way in helping us navigate the ups and downs of life, even in the most unexpected and unusual circumstances.

Confusing French Lesson

By Paul Carter

At the age of 15, I had already earned a notorious reputation for my challenging behaviour. The school had grown weary of my numerous disciplinary reports, and it seemed that each incident was another straw weighing down the proverbial camel's back. Little did I know that the final straw was waiting for me in a place far from what I had known before – Cornwall.

My family's decision to relocate to Cornwall was a fresh start, an opportunity to leave behind the negative influences and behaviours that had plagued my adolescence. As we settled into our new life, I found myself enrolled in a new school, eager to make a positive impression.

On my very first day, the excitement of new beginnings was shattered during my French lesson. The atmosphere in the classroom was filled with anticipation as the teacher, Mr Cooper, introduced himself and began explaining the importance of showing respect to one another.

As the lesson continued, I listened intently, my mind racing with thoughts of how to make a fresh start. Suddenly, Mr Cooper called on me to answer a question. I hesitated for a moment, and then I decided to speak my mind, believing that honesty was the key to building a strong foundation.

"Respect has to be earned," I blurted out, my words echoing through the room. The class fell silent, their eyes shifting towards me with a mix of surprise and curiosity.

Mr Cooper's face contorted into a mix of surprise and mild outrage. "Young man, that is highly disrespectful. You will have to see the headmaster immediately," he exclaimed firmly.

Confusion swirled in my mind. How could speaking the truth be disrespectful? Wasn't it important to have open discussions about these matters? Despite my confusion, I followed his instructions and made my way to the headmaster's office, uncertain of what awaited me.

I knocked hesitantly on the door and entered the office, where I found myself face-to-face with a stern-looking headmaster. Mr Thomas, the headmaster, gestured for me to sit down, his expression a mix of curiosity and concern.

"I've been informed about the incident in your French class," Mr Thomas began, his voice calm yet authoritative. "While I understand your perspective, it's important to recognise that respect can manifest in different ways.

The incident in my French class became a turning point in my journey towards personal growth. It taught me the significance of effective communication, empathy, and the value of embracing different perspectives. With time, my reputation transformed, and I became known not for my challenging behaviour but for my willingness to learn, adapt, and respect the boundaries of those around me.

Finding Myself: From Career Uncertainty to ADHD Diagnosis

By Andy Gonzalez

I found myself in yet another new job. It was almost funny how frequently I found myself in this situation, grappling with the uncertainty of my career path well into my twenties. The concept of finding something and sticking with it continued to taunt me, making me question my choices and abilities. This time, I was entering the world of banking, doing my best to push through the month-long training I dreaded every day.

Among the other trainees, there was one I started conversing with when I happened to sit beside him. He was of a similar age, and his distinctive speech pattern bore an uncanny resemblance to the legendary Jack Nicholson. One day, I happened to mention my struggle with staying awake during the seemingly endless training sessions. During this discussion, he dropped a bombshell that would eventually alter my perception of myself.

He confided that he had once battled the same issue, and his solution had been somewhat unconventional. He visited a psychiatrist and feigned symptoms of ADHD to secure a prescription for Adderall, presumably for recreational purposes. Curious, I pressed for details, imagining him putting on an absurd display to convince the psychiatrist of his supposed condition.

What he described, however, turned out to be a mirror reflecting my own behaviour.

The traits he mentioned – getting up randomly, interrupting conversations, and struggling to retain information – felt strangely familiar, like pieces of a puzzle falling into place. I couldn't shake the feeling that the way he mimicked ADHD symptoms was not all that different from how I navigated through my daily life.

I began researching more about ADHD and its manifestations in adulthood. The deeper I delved into the topic, the more it felt like I was reading about myself. After persistent effort, I managed to secure an appointment with a psychiatrist who specialized in ADHD.

Sitting in the psychiatrist's office, I expressed my concerns and answered her questions. The evaluation process was thorough, and without much delay, the psychiatrist delivered the diagnosis – "severe adult ADHD." I was surprised, though not entirely. I felt relief because there was finally an explanation for my challenges, but it was still a blow. Here was professional confirmation that something was wrong with me. The "ADHD" part didn't catch me entirely by surprise, but the "severe" aspect stung a bit.

Leaving the psychiatrist's office with a prescription for medication, I also had an entirely new perception of myself. I was sad, but more than that, I was hopeful. Finally, I knew that I wasn't just lazy or weak-willed. I had a condition that was not my fault. Now, I could learn to deal with it and hopefully find peace and accomplishment in my life. I also had much hope in the prescription, but that ultimately wasn't the answer to all my problems that I hoped it would be. I went through several different medications before I finally learned that stimulants, while great for some, were not for me.

Today, I am on a prescription that helps me focus when I need to without changing who I am, for which I am grateful because it turns out I like who I am. Sure, I make many mistakes that other people don't. Yes, many things take me longer than the average person. But I also have many skills that the average person would envy. My lack of specialisation has taught me that I can adapt to almost any situation. I may not be the professional I once wished I was, but I am valued for my flexibility and the variety of talents I have accumulated. I have become accustomed to being the Swiss army knife wherever I go, and I don't plan to change.

I am grateful I met that drug-swingling coworker during that training. That chance encounter led to a path of self-discovery I never imagined. Since then, I have changed careers three times, and I may change it again in the future. Who knows? All I do know is that I look forward to finding out.

"Don't watch the clock; do what it does. Keep going"

-Sam Levenson-

Life Happens When You Least Expect It

By Cynthia Hammer

My story might not be funny, but if you have ADHD and cause expensive trouble, my story will make you feel better. My ADHD secret superpower is to turn everyday tasks into memorable disasters. I was told long ago by another ADHDer that if you can laugh about it later, you can laugh about it now. I am not quite ready to do that as I write this story ten minutes after I finished cleaning up, as best I could, the mess I caused.

I have allergies, so I do a daily nasal rinse. I hate rinsing my nose with cold water, but I hate wasting water by letting it run long enough to get hot. I had the brilliant idea of using a heating coil to warm up the water. When I want warm water for my nasal rinse, I fill up the Pyrex cup that sits on the sink with water, insert the plugged-in heating coil, and wait a few moments for the water to warm.

As I worked peacefully in my office next to the bathroom, the tranquil silence was shattered by a noise as loud as a jackhammer, followed by the sound of shattering glass. My husband, Steve, yelled from downstairs, "Are you okay?" I called back, "Yes, but what was that noise?" It sounded like it was upstairs, but I didn't see anything out of place.

I shouted, "Maybe something fell over in the attic, but I can't think of anything that would. Perhaps it was something outside."

A short while later, I went downstairs to prepare dinner. While eating, I said, "Well, if we ever figure out what caused that noise, we will probably wish we had explored more for the cause." After dinner, I returned to my office to do more desk work.

Suddenly, the smoke alarm upstairs started ringing, although I mistakenly thought it was the smoke alarm in the kitchen. I thought, "Steve is there. He will take care of the problem and shut off the alarm." But the alarm kept ringing and didn't stop. I thought, "I bet Steve went outside, and the pot of water he put on the stove for his tea has gone dry. That is why the alarm is going off."

I rushed downstairs, but the downstairs smoke alarm wasn't ringing. It was open with the battery hanging down. I had turned it off a few days earlier when I burnt something and forgot to reset it. Confused, I wondered why the upstairs alarm was ringing.

My husband came in from outside. He, too, wondered why the upstairs alarm was ringing. I said, "There is no smoke. What is going on? Perhaps our house is haunted. First, some loud noise and the sound of glass breaking, then the smoke alarm goes off."

Steve came upstairs to explore. He smelled smoke. I hadn't smelled the smoke because I had lost my sense of smell years earlier following sinus surgery. He was astonished I couldn't smell the smoke. "You can't smell the smoke??" Every time, it seems, I must remind him. I can't smell.

He looked in the bathroom, and the culprit was unrecognisable. The glass cup was shattered like a mosaic masterpiece on the bathroom floor.

A particularly large piece of glass was glued to the sink, held fast in a glob of melted plastic, which was the former heating coil handle. The cord was charred and looked like the beginnings of a modern art installation. We were relieved to find the problem before it caused a fire.

The bathroom electricity had shut off. My husband went downstairs to reset it in the fuse box. After several minutes, when the coil, glass, and plastic had cooled, I cleaned up the mess. I gathered up the glass and, with some scraping, wiped up most of the plastic. Some bits proved difficult to remove and will require touch-up painting. But I thought I had gotten off easy. But after cleaning the sink, I realized I hadn't gotten away with only the loss of a $20 heating coil.

With a significant crack, the sink will be much more expensive to replace. I had a heating coil for a few months before I forgot it, left the bathroom, and returned later to notice it had melted. That time I simply unplugged the destroyed heating coil, discarded it, and decided not to tell Steve. He doesn't need to know I messed up again. Life is more pleasant for both of us when I employ "out of sight, out of mind." So, I buried the mangled heating coil deep in the trash so he wouldn't notice it.

I debated whether to buy another heating coil. "Would I forget again? No," I foolishly told myself. "I won't forget. I have learned my lesson. I won't leave the bathroom until I have unplugged it." I bought the new heating coil about a week ago! Now I tell myself, "No more heating coils, ever! It is wiser to waste water than to burn the house down."

"The only limit to our realisation of tomorrow will be our doubts of today."

-Franklin D. Roosevelt-

ADHD & Drama Success

By Abi Horsfield

Having ADHD is like tossing a coin; one side represents the superpowers enabling you to do so much more than others: creativity, relentless energy, and mental juggling. On the other side lies chaos, sleeplessness, lily pad brain, and boredom.

I hated being a child; I felt restricted and caged in. I was constantly having to adapt who I am to fit the circumstances I sit in. School was torture—wearing clothes that felt wrong, sitting still, listening, and shutting my mouth. When I left school, life began.

I truly believe that drama is what made me who I am. I am good at it, intuitive and creative, and able to see details others don't. I write, direct, and perform in plays. Improvisation comes naturally to me, and I bounce off other people's ideas. I have a great memory, and nothing gets past me. I am an accomplished facilitator who enthuses and encourages others to step outside their comfort zones in the safety of a workshop space.

Drama and facilitation have taken me around the world. I was a clown in Northern Ireland in the late 1980s. I lived in South Africa, working on projects that changed laws. I worked with disabled orphans in Bukhara, mediated conversations between warlords, and took a blue silk parachute into Abkhazia to help the children heal after the war ended. Last year, I received a distinction for my Master, which I completed in a year while working full-time for a Community Theatre Company.

But I think the biggest success story is being a mum. I am the ADHD single mother of an ASD child who is amazing, bright, academic, socially awkward, and funny. By some miracle, I have managed to feed him every day. I have found unconditional love, which has meant I stayed even when, at times, I am bored and restless. I have managed to get the washing out of the machine and dry it. I have become a warrior for Neurodiverse rights, fighting this corner, advocating on his behalf, and setting up with an ADHD friend, Willfulmisfits CIC, a Neurodiverse arts company so he and others like him can join a youth theatre. I have stopped taking as many risks, and despite our often 'clashes of the spangles,' we have gotten on great for the last 13 years.

My Diagnosis Transformed My Life

By Daley Jones

Once burdened by poor self-esteem, I found solace and purpose as a Police Officer in the Metropolitan Police. I quickly gravitated towards detective work, a path that suited my need for structure and the thrill of urgent cases requiring fast action. However, I soon realised that my brain, wired with ADHD, struggled when faced with tasks lacking immediacy. My brain fails to fire into gear. I know the task is important - I know it will directly benefit me – I have the time and means to complete it – But my brain will just say, "No, not important, not interested, what's in it for me?" This inevitably leads to stress at work and a feeling that you are lazy or incompetent.

But then came April 2021, the month of my ADHD diagnosis, and a newfound understanding of my struggles. It was a revelation that I was not lazy or incompetent but wired differently. Armed with this knowledge, I adopted a mindset that acknowledged my weaknesses and sought ways to manage them. I learned strategies that helped me navigate my work and became an advocate for my needs.

Fortunately, my workplace was blessed with a management team that understood and recognised my condition. They listened to my concerns and made an effort to comprehend the unique challenges I faced. This understanding became my greatest asset during the workday. It also highlighted the importance of comprehending one's work style and striving to find a role that aligns with personal strengths.

In my case, I realised that longer-term projects were not my forte, and I thrived in structured environments.

Since my diagnosis, I took the initiative to establish and co-chair a national police support group for individuals with ADHD. This group has grown to encompass 500 members, providing assistance and guidance to those navigating the complexities of ADHD. Additionally, I became a trustee of two ADHD charities, driven by a desire to pay forward the help and support I received.

With a newfound sense of self-esteem, I began embracing opportunities that I once believed were beyond my reach. I successfully passed my sergeants exam and secured a specialised role within the past year, achievements I previously thought were unattainable. Diagnosis has truly transformed my life, opening doors I never thought I deserved. And now, filled with hope and excitement, I eagerly await the future, eager to see what it holds for me.

ADHD, PTSD And My Military Career

By Carlos Rodriguez

Determined to pave my way to a brighter future, I approached the military recruitment office. Despite my passion and enthusiasm, I did not know I had ADHD, a condition that, according to regulations, would disqualify me from serving in the military.

With a sense of purpose burning within me, I enlisted in the military, believing I had signed up for a four-year commitment. I eagerly anticipated the day I would receive my full educational benefits, ready to seize the opportunities that awaited me. Little did I know, fate had other plans in store.

Years flew by, and I excelled in my military career. What I thought would be a mere stepping stone to education became a remarkable decade-long journey filled with accomplishments and personal growth.

In 2016, however, the burdens of my service started to take their toll. I began to experience flashbacks, nightmares, and emotional turmoil. I was caught in the grip of post-traumatic stress disorder (PTSD), much like the troubled actor Charlie Sheen had once famously gone through.

2018: I was diagnosed with Traumatic Brain Injury (TBI) due to a roadside explosion. The pieces of the puzzle started falling into place, shedding light on the invisible scars I had carried for so long.

Then, in 2019, another crucial diagnosis came to light: ADHD. I finally understood why I had faced challenges in my military career that others seemed to handle effortlessly.

It was a bittersweet revelation, as I now know the underlying cause of my previous struggles.

Through resilience and determination, I showed that overcoming adversity and pursuing personal growth was possible, despite seemingly insurmountable odds.

While my military career had taken an unexpected turn, I remained grateful for the opportunities it has provided me. The military has given me a sense of purpose, instilled valuable skills, and shaped me into the person I have become.

ADHD: Unleashing Life's Potential

By Liam Tuohy

For years, I had struggled with ADHD without even realising it. Every day was a battle, as I found myself constantly getting into trouble and being expelled from one school after another. Holding down a job seemed impossible, and a sense of hopelessness overshadowed my dreams.

However, fate had a surprising twist in store for me. Approximately a year ago, I finally received the long-awaited diagnosis and was prescribed medication that would profoundly transform my life. With the help of my medications, I began to experience the world in a different light. My scattered thoughts gradually became more focused, and my impulsive behaviours started to reduce. It was like a fog had lifted, revealing a more straightforward path to my success.

With my mind finally working in harmony, my life took an extraordinary turn. No longer confined by my previous limitations, I set out to achieve the unimaginable. Fuelled by determination and the desire to make a difference, I pursued my passion for fitness. I founded my own fitness company 2Tuff Health and Fitness, a venture I once believed was beyond my reach.

This journey was not without its challenges. I have encountered numerous obstacles, but my perseverance has remained unwavering. The qualities that once led me astray were now harnessed as strengths.

My boundless energy became an asset in designing engaging workout routines, and my ability to think outside the box allowed me to create innovative fitness programs tailored to the unique needs of my clients.

My journey resonates with my clients, as they witnessed tangible proof that even the most challenging obstacles can be overcome with the right support and determination.

Looking ahead, I can envision a future brimming with possibilities. My once turbulent path has led me to a place of fulfilment and purpose. I am grateful for the diagnosis that finally shed light on my inner struggles, for without it, I may never have discovered the strength within me.

My journey from an undiagnosed individual battling ADHD to a thriving entrepreneur and beacon of hope is a testament to the transformative power of self-discovery and the importance of support. And as I step into the future, I am brimmed with anticipation, ready to face whatever challenges lay ahead, knowing I have the resilience to conquer them.

Epilogue

As we end this vibrant tapestry of personal journeys, successes, and the unbridled humour that often accompanies the intricate dance of life with ADHD, we find ourselves surrounded by a symphony of resilience and joy. The stories within these pages have illuminated the challenges of navigating a world wired differently and celebrated the triumphs that arise from embracing that uniqueness.

In this epilogue, we take a moment to revel in the shared laughter and applause that resound throughout these narratives. These adults with ADHD have repeatedly proven that humour is not only a coping mechanism but a potent tool for fostering connections, breaking down barriers, and unearthing the bright side even amid chaos.

As we've journeyed alongside these individuals, we've witnessed the sheer determination that fuels their successes – the ability to transform obstacles into opportunities and setbacks into stepping stones. Through their stories, we've learned that while the path might be unconventional, it is brimming with unexpected detours that often lead to the most beautiful destinations.

Their tales are a testament to the power of seeing life through a different lens – one that captures the nuances, the quirks, and the idiosyncrasies that make each moment a rich tapestry of colour. We've celebrated the moments of hyperfocus that allow for dazzling creativity and productivity, and we've chuckled at the tales of forgetfulness that have led to hilarious mix-ups and misadventures.

But beyond the laughter, there is a profound sense of accomplishment that resonates in these stories. From seemingly small victories like organising a cluttered desk to monumental achievements like launching a successful business, these individuals have shown that anything is possible with determination, support, and a healthy dose of humour.

As you turn the final pages of this book, remember that the spirit of these stories lives on – not just in the words printed on these pages, but in the resilience you carry forward. May you be inspired by the successes, buoyed by the laughter, and fortified by the unwavering determination that has shaped the lives of these remarkable individuals.

And as you navigate the twists and turns of your journey, may you find comfort in the shared experiences of those who have walked a similar path. May you always remember that amidst the challenges, an abundance of resilience, creativity, and laughter is waiting to be unearthed.

So go forth with a heart full of humour, a spirit ignited by triumphs, and a mind open to the possibilities that arise when you embrace your unique ADHD journey. The stories within these pages are not just the conclusion of a book – they are the opening notes of a new chapter in your own story, infused with humour, resilience, and the vibrant colours of a life well-lived.

Directory of Co-Authors and Contributors

Bernadette Ashton
ADHD Lancashire
www.adhdlancashire.com

Rachael Beatie
Nuro-Boost
www.transformwithrachael.teachable.com

Jen Bee
Baddass Coaching
www.baddasscoaching.com

Andrea Bilbow OBE
ADDISS UK
www.addiss.co.uk

Alan Brown
ADDCrusher™
www.addcrusher.com

Alison Clink
Dundee & Angus ADHD Support Group
www.adhddasupport.org

Tony Coward
Nomadd Coaching
www.nomadd.coach

Cynthia Hammer
Inattentive ADHD Coalition
www.iadhd.org

James Hansen
JH Counselling Solutions
www.jameshansen.co.uk

Jan Hanson
Difference in the Making
www.differenceinthemaking.com

Jenny Haslam
Create your own success
www.createyourownsuccess.co.uk

Natasha Hickling
Indigo Hub
www.indigo-hub.com

Beverley Nolker
ADHD Awesome Coaching
www.adhdawesomecoaching.com

Chris Maddocks
Attentive Apparel
www.attentiveapparel.com

Steve McLaughlin
Stiddard Wealth
www.stiddardwealth.com

Emily Nuttall
Emily Nuttall
https://linktr.ee/emilyn93

Kimberley Pereira
ADHD Coach CT
www.adhdcoachct.com

Robert Powell
DB Powell Repairs
www.powellrepairs.co.uk

Emma Sails
Emma Sails Coaching
www.emmasailscoaching.com

Kim Sheppard
Kim-e-Fleurs
www.kim-e-fleurs.co.uk

Bethany Thomas
Unbound Mind
www.unboundmindadhdlifecoaching.com

Liam Tuohy
ADHD Fitness Coach
www.adhdfitnesscoach.com

About the Creator of this book

Bernadette Ashton is the remarkable Founder and Director of ADHD Lancashire! With nearly two decades of experience advocating for ADHD and holding the title of Certified ADHD Life Coach, Bernadette's expertise and passion shine through in the way she supports families and adults dealing with ADHD. Her deep understanding and empathy make her work truly stand out.

What makes Bernadette's journey even more unique is her personal experience, having lived through over 50 years in a neurodiverse family that includes ADHD, Dyslexia, and Autism. These experiences have given her incredible insights that she's eager to share with others. Bernadette's story is a testament to her unwavering determination and resilience.

Bernadette has spent many years running her own businesses, ranging from mobile phones, telephone systems, and computers to ladies' fashions. Recently, she has also been involved in education, training, and coaching for adults with ADHD and Autism.

In 2005, Bernadette's son embarked on a challenging journey of diagnoses that included ADHD, dyslexia, autism and learning difficulties.

This became the turning point that led Bernadette to a deep exploration of neurodiversity. With nothing but an unbreakable internet connection, she dove into the mysteries of the neurodiverse world, much like Sherlock Holmes. She also delved into the realm of Special Educational Needs for her son.

From there, Bernadette threw herself into learning with boundless enthusiasm, achieving many neurodiverse qualifications. By 2011, she had become the driving force behind ADHD Lancashire, a safe haven of support for families walking the same path. She brought together parents of neurodiverse children, organising meetings and social gatherings that provided comfort, companionship, and heartfelt understanding. Her own experiences as a parent of a neurodiverse child fuelled her determination to break down the barriers of isolation.

2013 Destiny introduced her to Dean, a partner who shared her mission. Together, they established an Adult Support Group, their collaboration resembling that of partners, complementing each other seamlessly. Their joint efforts, whether through virtual interactions or face-to-face meetings, created a community within the neurodiverse world. They stood ready to support people through the process of diagnosis and to face any challenge that came their way.

These support group sessions are held twice a month and provide a fantastic opportunity for like-minded adults to connect and confront life's challenges head-on. Among the unwavering support and genuine camaraderie, laughter flourished, resulting in humorous stories that left attendees in stitches, metaphorically and sometimes even literally.

Bernadette's insatiable thirst for knowledge led her to attend a three-day ADHD conference in Liverpool organised by ADDISS, a national charity for families with ADHD. This serendipitous encounter introduced her to a global community of ADHD advocates and experts united by their determination to make a difference.

One particularly memorable event during the conference was the uproarious "ADHD Got Talent" night, where the display of talent rivalled even the wittiest jesters. Amidst all the serious discussions, this event stood out as a pure celebration of joy and amusement.

Bernadette's journey continued to ascend as she got involved with ADDISS, eventually becoming a trustee and helping to organise ADHD Conference tours across the UK.

In this role, she supported ADDISS with their conferences and embarked on a whirlwind tour that left participants satisfied and new connections forged within the ADHD community.

Her ambitions even took her across continents, attending ADHD events in cities like Glasgow, Athens, Malaga, Manchester, London, and beyond. As her portfolio expanded, she undertook training to become a Certified ADHD Life Coach through the International ADHD Coach Training Center in America. She also has accomplished her International Coaching Federation ACC qualification. Today, she utilises her skills to guide her adult ADHD clients towards success by helping them understand and overcome their challenges.

Embracing her role as a mentor, Bernadette extended her expertise to lead ADHD courses for adults, parents, and professionals.

Her courses, presentations, and workshops uncover the intricacies and strengths of ADHD, leaving participants with newfound clarity and determination.

Fuelled by boundless enthusiasm, Bernadette is on a mission to break down the walls of isolation and misunderstanding for all those navigating the world of ADHD. A well of knowledge, humour, and empathy, Bernadette serves as an inspiration and a source of camaraderie.

In an unexpected turn of events in 2023, Bernadette crossed paths with a publisher at a networking event, leading to a transformative proposition. The idea of writing a book initially met her characteristic modesty, considering her dyslexia. However, the wealth of stories from her support group and the people she met on her ADHD journey sparked a creative idea – a collaborative book.

And so, the seed of innovation was planted, blossoming into a vision of a book filled with neurodiverse wit and warmth, woven together collaboratively by extraordinary individuals living with adult ADHD. This concept promises to become a unique gem, ready to capture the ADHD community's attention with laughter and inspiration.

Most notably, the upcoming book features a treasury of stories from Bernadette's diverse interactions, showcasing the achievements of a diverse array of individuals. Together, these stories create a symphony of joy and motivation, poised to make a lasting impact on the neurodiverse world.

Prepare to embark on a journey with Bernadette and her neurodiverse companions as they navigate the intricate tapestry of life's wonders. With unwavering determination, they are ready to reveal a narrative infused with resilience, humour, and the unconquerable human spirit.

ADHD Lancashire Services

www.adhdlancashire.com

Adult Support Group Meetings

We totally understand that ADHD can have a significant impact on all aspects of your life and sometimes leave you feeling isolated. But worry not because our support group is here to bring you the understanding and connection you need!

Joining our meetings is a fantastic way to connect with like-minded individuals who face similar challenges. We've got some exciting guest speakers lined up for our meetings, so you'll get to hear from experts in the field, too!

www.adhdlancashire.com/adult-adhd-meetings

Private Facebook Group

Come and join other like-minded adults at various stages of their ADHD journeys. We share a wealth of information, updates and tips, and you can ask other members any questions.

www.facebook.com/groups/adultadhdsupportgroup

Private ADHD Coaching Sessions

Bernadette is not only a Certified ADHD Life Coach but has also earned her ACC International Coaching Federation accreditation.

Her expertise and dedication shine through in how she supports families and adults with ADHD, bringing a deep understanding and empathy to her work.

Her personal journey adds a unique perspective, having lived through over 50 years in a neurodiverse family that includes ADHD, Dyslexia, and Autism. These experiences have given her invaluable insights that she is eager to share with others.

We offer several coaching packages and group coaching will be available soon.

https://www.adhdlancashire.com/adhdcoaching

ADHD Essentials Eight-week Group Coaching Programme

Affordable and Impactful ADHD Coaching Solutions

We are delighted to offer you the opportunity to participate in impactful weekly small-group coaching at a significantly more affordable cost. We have several groups to choose from.

https://www.adhdlancashire.com/groupcoaching

ADHD & Positive Parenting Solutions Course

Parenting doesn't have to be a battle. Come and learn how to effectively use a toolkit of strategies to help manage unwanted behaviour and encourage positive behaviours. This programme will work with all children, so it's ideal if your child has siblings.

www.adhdlancashire.com/parent-adhd-course

Professional and Teacher training

We can offer various ADHD awareness training to organisations and schools tailored to your needs.

If you require any bespoke training around ADHD in the classroom or workplace, please contact us with your requirements

https://www.adhdlancashire.com/adhd-courses

bernadette@adhdlancashire.com

Printed in Great Britain
by Amazon